# IT'S
# A WRAP II
## sewing new shapes,
## exploring new techniques

### susan breier

*Martingale*®
& COMPANY

## Credits

President & CEO ✳ Tom Wierzbicki

Editor in Chief ✳ Mary V. Green

Managing Editor ✳ Tina Cook

Technical Editor ✳ Dawn Anderson

Copy Editor ✳ Sheila Chapman Ryan

Design Director ✳ Stan Green

Production Manager: Regina Girard

Illustrator ✳ Laurel Strand

Cover & Text Designer ✳ Shelly Garrison

Photographer ✳ Brent Kane

## Mission Statement

Dedicated to providing quality products
and service to inspire creativity.

It's a Wrap II:
Sewing New Shapes, Exploring New Techniques

© 2010 by Susan Breier

That Patchwork Place® is an imprint of
Martingale & Company®.

Martingale & Company
19021 120th Ave. NE, Ste 102
Bothell, WA 98011-9511 USA
www.martingale-pub.com

Printed in China
15 14 13 12 11 10          8 7 6 5 4 3 2

**Library of Congress Cataloging-in-Publication Data is
available upon request.**

ISBN: 978-1-56477-931-1

## DEDICATION

To fellow sewing enthusiasts: A seed has been planted in all of us and it's there for a reason. It needs to be nurtured and it's meant to grow. It's our gift—our special talent.

Search out and develop that talent. Our first attempts toward that goal may be difficult but don't be discouraged. Nothing good ever came easy.

The ability to sew needs to be passed on. Please take the time to share your talent, your gift of sewing, so that others will reap the rewards of creating something wonderful with fabric.

## ACKNOWLEDGMENTS

Thank you to my husband, Jeffrey; our sons, Christopher and Scott; and their families. You are my reason for being, my reason to carry on with life in the hope of touching people in a helpful way.

I truly value the role that Martingale & Company has played in my life by publishing and promoting my ideas. A special thank-you to Dawn Anderson, who edited both of my books.

And finally to you, my friends through sewing: your response to my first book has been incredible. I appreciate all of your positive comments and hope that you find this book equally inspiring.

# CONTENTS

# ɔNTRODUCTION

It's time to share some new ideas for wrapping clothesline with you. May your spirits be lifted by using this simple method as a guide to creating your very own unique projects. Making wrapped and coiled projects provides a relaxing break from the sewing projects many of us are used to. I started creating wrapped and coiled projects about seven years ago and here I am still stitching the fun stuff.

What's kept me fascinated for so long with wrapping, coiling, and zigzag stitching? It's the chance to change my mind while the projects are still under construction. Oval baskets can turn into purses, small plates can become large pieces of art, and embellishments can change everything. No design plan is set in concrete.

I mix new fabric and leftover scraps with clothesline to create whatever project interests me at the time. It could be a basket, a purse, a wall hanging, or a place mat. The opportunity to make changes during the construction stage gives me a natural high. There's excitement in the air. Perhaps it's something only a person who loves to handle and stitch fabric can understand. If you've paged through this book, I bet you know exactly what I mean.

The projects in this book are designed for all skill levels and are sewn on a regular sewing machine—not the top of the line, and not an industrial machine. My machine has an open-arm option, and for the largest projects I add an extension table, but most of the projects can be created without these features.

Reading "Basic Techniques" on page 10 will prepare you to create projects of your very own design, not just duplicate mine. Allow my projects to be your inspiration and guide, but let your creativity shine through. With all the possibilities for shaping the projects; adding handles and embellishments; plus customizing sizes, colors, and lids; and choosing from the vast amount of fabric out there…why, the choices can make my heart skip a beat!

Any sewer familiar with my first book, *It's a Wrap*, will find fresh ideas to try here, with three new project shapes, including a triangle, a heart, and a figure-eight basket—complete with lids. You'll also find tips for working with synthetic fabrics and for creating your own coordinating fabrics through color enhancement. Because the purses are so popular, I've also included a new purse design for you to try. Have fun!

# GENERAL MATERIALS

All the baskets, bowls, and purses in this book are created from clothesline and fabric using simple wrapping and coiling methods and zigzag stitching. Most projects can be made from just a few materials and minimal tools and equipment. For purses, you may need handle or closure hardware in addition to the regular supplies. You also may want to have a selection of embellishment materials on hand. Below is a list of the items most often required.

## FABRIC

The best fabric for most projects is 100%-cotton fabric that's been prewashed. Avoid bulky fabrics such as flannel, denim, and decorator fabrics. Also avoid loosely woven fabric, such as linen, because it will fray too much. Multicolored prints look great and hide mistakes better than solid colors. Batiks work wonderfully; because of their higher thread count, they don't fray very much. These projects are ideal for using up leftover scraps. Ugly fabrics and prints that you wouldn't normally pick out are fine if the colors are right. The fabric designs change in the sewing process because of the wrapping, and part of the fun is to see a new pattern emerge.

Although cotton fabric is the easiest to work with, it's possible to create some spectacular projects using synthetics. For synthetics that have a tendency to unravel, I back the fabric with a fusible web, such as Pellon's Wonder-Under. The fusible web helps stabilize the fabric and prevents excessive fraying. It is a good idea to test a small sample before preparing all of the fabric. If the synthetic fabric is too sheer the clothesline will show through. For sheer fabrics, you can try cutting the strips a little wider and overlapping them more to conceal the clothesline. If an 80 universal needle doesn't produce even stitches on your synthetic sample, try a ballpoint or a metallic needle. You may also need to adjust your tension. Don't be afraid to experiment. If you have some unusual fabrics in your stash or a garment that you'd like to recycle, why not try wrapping and coiling it into a spectacular-looking project, like the one shown below. Also see pages 73 and 74 for two additional synthetic baskets.

To prepare synthetic fabrics prone to fraying for the wrapping and coiling method, apply fusible web to the wrong side of the fabric, following the manufacturer's instructions. I use a pressing sheet on top of the fabric and another underneath to help prevent the fabric from

This shining 2¼"-high oval basket is made with silver metallic mesh. For this project, I cut the fabric strips 1" wide because of excess unraveling and I overlapped the wrapping more to hide the clothesline. I also added silver cording around the wrapping to encourage the mesh strips to stay in place. Other colors of metallic cording were used in the 1¼" band where the seed beads are stitched. Gray thread was used for the zigzag stitching.

discoloring. Leave the paper backing on the fusible web and cut the strips following "Cutting Fabric Strips" on page 11. Remove the paper backing just before wrapping the clothesline (see "Wrapping Clothesline with Fabric Strips" on page 12). Wrapping clothesline with fusible-web-backed fabric is different from wrapping with cotton. The web may tear or twist, but just cover the clothesline the best that you can. When you zigzag stitch it in place and trim any visible web, you will end up with a unique basket.

Fabric yardages are given for the main projects in the book. Use the yardages listed below as a guideline for creating your own baskets. In most cases, the yardage listed is generous. Depending on the width of the fabric strips used for wrapping and how closely the wraps are made, it should take about a 22" length of fabric to cover about 1' of clothesline.

## Yardage Guidelines

- 1¾ yards of fabric for a large purse
- 1½ yards of fabric for a medium purse
- 1¼ yards of fabric for a small purse
- 1½ yards of fabric for a large basket or bowl with a lid
- 1¼ yards of fabric for a small or medium basket or bowl with a lid
- 1 yard of fabric for a large basket or bowl
- ¾ yard of fabric for a small or medium basket or bowl
- ¾ yard of fabric for an 11" to 12" plate

## BASIC SUPPLIES

The items listed below are frequently used in making the projects shown in this book. Additional embellishment supplies may also be required, depending on the project you choose to make.

**Adhesives.** Following is a list of adhesives I've used with good results. Test the glue on scrap fabric first. If it doesn't dry clear, use it sparingly, especially on dark fabrics, where excess glue will easily show. Always allow adequate drying time.

## Adhesives

- **Crafter's Pick Fabric Glue.** This glue is able to hold flat buttons and glass beads in place. It has proven itself to hold fabric handles and purse pockets securely with only a few hand-tacking stitches as reinforcement.

- **E-6000 Craft Adhesive.** This glue comes in a tube and is another quick fix when machine stitching is too difficult. Hand tack after applying.

- **Fabric glue stick (acid free).** This type of glue is used for securing the fabric to the clothesline and for holding some embellishments in place until they can be stitched permanently.

- **Fray Check.** Use Fray Check to secure threads after hand stitching embellishments, such as buttons and beads, to a project.

- **Iron-on adhesive.** Use your favorite fusible web or HeatnBond Lite for fusible appliqués. Use HeatnBond Ultra Hold for creating curled embellishments such as flowers and streamers (see "Dimensional-Fabric Embellishments" on page 65).

- **Mighty Mendit Permanent Bonding Agent.** This adhesive works great and is a real time-saver for securing handles and purse pockets with minimal hand tacking. It dries fast but will show on your fabric if you use an excessive amount.

- **Ross Glue Pen.** A bright yellow cap makes it easy to find this tall, clear tube of glue. I use this as a sealer on the top rim of a project to help hold the last row of stitching and any fraying in place. Just use your fingers to spread after applying. It's available at many office-supply stores or where school supplies are sold. This product always dries clear and adds a bit of stiffness.

- **Tacky glue.** Use Aleene's Original Tacky Glue or Clear Gel Tacky Glue to secure large embellishments or handles in place before hand sewing them permanently.

GENERAL MATERIALS

- **Two-step clear epoxy glue.** Use this adhesive for attaching embellishments that can't be stitched to the project. Do a test sample first. I generally use the drying time to determine which epoxy to use. The longer the drying time the better it seems to hold.

**Closure hardware.** If you're making a purse, use the hardware of your choice or one package of Velcro.

**Clothesline.** I recommend ³⁄₁₆" poly-reinforced cotton clothesline. You will use about 15 yards for an 11½" plate and 30 yards or less for a small or medium basket. Large baskets could take 50 yards or more. A medium purse requires about 100 yards. See "Resources" on page 79 for more information about suitable types of clothesline. Not all types of clothesline are sewing machine friendly.

**Fabric stiffener.** Use Aleene's or Crafter's Pick fabric stiffener to add support when needed. It can be applied to the entire project, just a lid, or just an embellishment. I often use it to help set the shape of a project. See "Preventing Floppy Baskets" on page 25 for more information.

**Purse handles.** A variety of purse handles are available at craft and fabric stores. Instructions for creative self-made handles are shown on page 45.

**Sewing-machine oil and cleaning brush.** Oil your bobbin case after eight hours of sewing and brush it out regularly; these can be very linty projects! Dispose of any machine oil that has darkened and buy new.

**Tape.** Use tape to mark a point on the base of the project where changes will occur. I use green or blue painter's tape or masking tape, all of which can be easily removed.

**Thread.** Select a 40- to 50-weight thread that will either match or blend with the fabrics used. I sometimes change colors to match certain areas of the project so that the zigzag stitching is less visible. I use black thread on very scrappy projects.

# TOOLS AND EQUIPMENT

**Acrylic extension table.** If you're using an open-arm sewing machine, place an acrylic extension table (available at sewing and quilt shops) next to the machine to create a level surface on which to rest the project while stitching. Or, you can create your own extension surface by stacking books next to the arm of the machine until the stack reaches the height of the arm. Be sure the surface is flat and level, because any change in the angle of the project under the needle will change the shape of the project. Although small and medium projects can be sewn without this aid, an extension table helps maintain the correct angle positions when sewing larger items.

**Appliqué foot or a zigzag foot.** An appliqué or zigzag foot allows easy viewing of the area being stitched.

**Cutting tools.** A rotary cutter, cutting mat, and clear ruler with a printed grid are needed for cutting fabric strips. Scissors will also be necessary.

**Hand-sewing needles.** A variety of needle sizes is useful. Needles are used for attaching embellishments and handles. Some areas must be sewn by hand because a sewing machine is unable to handle the bulk. A #9 milliner's needle is a good choice for hand sewing through layers.

**Iron and ironing board.** Use an iron and ironing board to press bindings or add embellishments with fusible web. There is no need to iron the fabric before rotary cutting your strips (unless it is very wrinkled). Slight wrinkles won't be visible on your wrapped clothesline. A mini-iron works great for fusing appliqués or pressing in small areas.

**Machine needles.** Use new #80 or #90 universal or Sharp sewing-machine needles. These work well for zigzag stitching rows of clothesline together. Change the needle if your thread breaks often or after every second project.

**Measuring tape.** This is handy for measuring clothesline and your project's width, length, and height.

**Needle-nose pliers.** Use these to pull hand-sewing needles through bulky areas of the project when attaching embellishments, pockets, or handles.

**Sewing machine.** I use an open-arm machine with a dual-feed feature. A standard machine that has a straight stitch and a zigzag-stitch feature will work well for making most of the projects shown in this book. The ability to drop the feed dogs is also helpful. Dropping the feed dogs allows bulky clothesline to be easily placed under the presser foot. Remember to return the feed dogs to their original position before sewing. Not all machines will produce exactly the same results since each machine is different. Experimentation is the key.

**Stiletto or bamboo stick.** Either of these tools helps move the project along without getting your fingers too close to the needle. The tools also help hold areas in position when sewing.

**Straight pins.** These are used to hold glued clothesline in place until dry or to hold embellishments in place while hand sewing.

**Teflon pressing sheet.** Using a pressing sheet will prevent fusible adhesives from coming in contact with your iron. It also helps prevent fabric embellishments from scorching.

**Walking foot.** A walking foot may be needed depending on how easily the wrapped clothesline moves along under the presser foot.

# BASIC TECHNIQUES

If you have fabrics in your stash and you're not sure what to do with them, consider using them to make a wrapped and coiled project. I have discovered that a little bit of paint or ink applied to a fabric can give it new life. I share some of my techniques in this chapter.

Once you understand the basic wrapping, coiling, and stitching techniques and the methods used for shaping a project, it will be easy to start designing your own pieces. Keep in mind that medium-sized projects are the easiest to make.

## ENHANCING FABRICS WITH PAINT

Wrapped and coiled projects are good for using up leftover fabrics. If you don't have a coordinating fabric in just the right color, you can easily modify fabrics with a little paint or ink to make perfect coordinates. The designs you apply to the fabric don't need to be perfect, because the fabric will be cut into narrow strips and take on a new appearance as the strips are wrapped around the clothesline. Try one of the following methods to give an old fabric new life.

Use fabrics that are 100% cotton or a cotton blend. Prepare your fabric for accepting the paint or ink by

first washing, drying, and ironing it. Do not use fabric softeners. Before applying color to the fabric, protect your clothing and cover your work surface.

**Stamping.** Inexpensive foam or rubber stamps with simple designs are great for applying ink or paint to fabrics. VersaCraft fabric inkpads were used to make these samples. Press a stamp onto the inkpad and transfer it to your fabric. To use dimensional paint or acrylic paints instead of ink, brush the paint onto the stamp in a thin layer, and then stamp it onto your fabric. Let the fabric dry, and then heat set the paint, following the manufacturer's instructions.

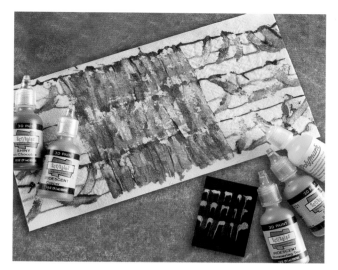

**Dimensional Fabric Paint.** Dimensional fabric paint is inexpensive and adds bold color and texture. Whatever brand you choose, look for "nontoxic" on the product packaging. Scribbles and Polymark paints were used for these samples but are only two of the popular brands. My eight-year-old grandson, Gavin Breier, made the muslin sample and used a brush to distribute the color. What fun! This fabric was used to make the light-colored stripes in the purse on page 42.

For the best sewing results, apply the paint so it's thinner than intended. To use this method, squeeze the paint from the applicator bottle directly onto the fabric. Distribute the paint with a thin brush, either immediately or as the paint is drying, for different effects. Avoid thick areas of paint that could be difficult to sew through. Let the paint dry. Heat setting isn't normally required.

**Shiva Paintstik.** Shiva Paintstiks add color to mostly solid fabrics. They're real oil paint formed into solid permanent sticks. A self-healing film is removed from the top of the stick to reveal a usable portion of drawable paint. You could make patterns with rubbing plates, but for the projects in this book you can just scribble lines on the fabric if you wish. Let the fabric dry for 24 hours. Follow the manufacturer's instructions for clean up and heat setting the fabric.

# CUTTING FABRIC STRIPS

Colorful strips of fabric are all that is needed to transform ordinary white clothesline into something decorative. It isn't necessary to cut the fabric strips perfectly. It's OK if part of the strip is narrower than another part or if the strips aren't on grain. Because the strips are wrapped around the clothesline, any miscuts will not be apparent.

Cut fabric strips from the full width of the fabric, folding the two selvage edges together and adjusting so that the fabric hangs straight. Fold again, bringing the fold to meet the selvages, so that you have four layers of fabric. Place the fabric on a cutting mat and position a clear ruler with a printed grid perpendicular to the fold. Because I only eyeball the width as I cut strips, I place the ruler on the fabric rather than on the mat. This gives me better control. Using a rotary cutter, make a straight cut across the fabric at one edge. Continue cutting the folded fabric into strips that measure about ½" to ¾" wide by the width of the fabric. Cut about 10 strips at a time to prevent fraying from handling.

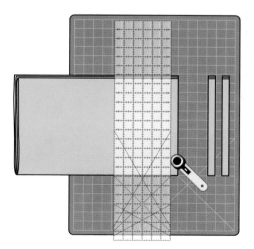

To cut strips from scrap pieces of fabric, cut the strips ½" to ¾" wide and as long as your scrap piece allows. Don't bother with lengths less than 3". It doesn't matter if the pieces are cut on the bias, crosswise grain, or lengthwise grain; however, cutting on a slight bias will reduce fraying at the edges. Fabric strips can also be torn, but this technique might produce fraying.

# WRAPPING CLOTHESLINE WITH FABRIC STRIPS

1. Make a straight cut at the end of the clothesline to eliminate any frayed ends. Use a glue stick to apply glue to both the end of the clothesline and to the first 1" of the wrong side of the fabric strip. Position the clothesline on the glued portion of the strip as shown, allowing ¼" of the fabric to extend beyond the end of the clothesline. Don't fold the excess fabric allowance over the end of the clothesline. It should remain flat with no clothesline inside. This ¼" area helps to fill the very center of the coil as the project is formed.

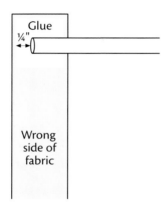

2. Wrap the fabric strip around the clothesline at an angle so that each wrap covers the edge and part of the previous wrap. Use a straight pin to hold the fabric in place at the starting point. Avoid placing the wraps too close together. Always wrap the fabric in the same direction, because changing the direction will show in the finished project. I use the "up, over, and under" wrap, which simply means I wrap the strip from the bottom side of the clothesline and up over the top of the clothesline, and then under the bottom of the clothesline. There is no need to pull tightly; just allow the fabric to firmly encircle the clothesline.

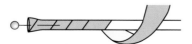

Glue the fabric in place about every 5" or when you feel it's necessary. Overlap the end with another fabric strip, pin, and keep wrapping. Always glue and pin the beginning and ending of each strip in place. When you have about 8" wrapped and the end is glued and pinned, straight stitch down the middle of the clothesline for the first 5" to prevent the fabric from unwrapping at the starting point. If you have difficulty moving the clothesline under the presser foot, refer to "Sewing Guidelines" on page 13. Remove the sewn length from the machine and trim the thread tails.

3. Continue wrapping the clothesline with fabric strips in the same manner until the desired amount of clothesline has been covered. It's best to wrap only a few feet of clothesline at a time. When you need more wrapped clothesline during the construction of a project, simply stop sewing 1" before the end of the wrapping with the needle down. Then, secure additional strips of fabric around the clothesline by gluing, wrapping, and pinning as before. Remove the pins as you come to them. Wrapping too far ahead leads to fraying and tangling of the line.

## Time-Saving Wrapping Trick

If the wrapping strips fray a bit, you might not have to trim all the loose threads. Simply choose the least frayed side of the strip and wrap the clothesline with that edge to the outside. The edge with the most fraying will be concealed as the clothesline is wrapped, hiding the loose threads under the layers of wrapping.

To produce a swirling effect, choose a striped fabric and cut strips across the striped pattern. Wrap the strips around the clothesline, always wrapping in the same direction. I use the "up, over, and under" wrap, opposite, to create a uniform look.

Round Bowl with Swirling Stripes

## JOINING TWO LENGTHS OF CLOTHESLINE

Most projects use one piece of clothesline that's long enough for the whole project. After making a few projects, you'll have various lengths of clothesline left over. Don't throw them out—they can be put together very easily to form usable lengths.

To join two lengths of clothesline, first cut about a 16" length of thread in a color that won't show through the fabric strip you plan to use for wrapping. Set the thread aside. Cut the ends of the clothesline that are to be joined so they're straight. Apply fabric glue stick to the end of each piece for 1"; overlap the ends for about ¼" to ½" and hold them together along the glued area. While holding the two pieces of clothesline together, tightly wrap the 16" length of thread around the joined ends, beginning about ¼" before the overlap and ending about ¼" beyond the overlap. While the glue is still damp, wrap a fabric strip around the join, wrapping that area firmer than normal to make it conform in size to the regular width of the clothesline. If a bump is obvious, finger-press the area to reshape. Pin and zigzag stitch the area while the glue is damp. It should blend nicely with the remainder of the wrapped clothesline if you give that area a little extra attention.

## SEWING GUIDELINES

The projects in this book are created by stitching rows of fabric-wrapped clothesline together using a zigzag stitch. Each project starts with a coiled base (round, oval, square, triangle, heart, or figure-eight shaped) of wrapped clothesline. The project grows as each row is added.

Before starting a project, clean the bobbin case of the sewing machine (follow the instructions in your manual) and install a new #80 or #90 universal or Sharp needle. The needle should be good for a couple of projects, but if your thread starts breaking or you have stitching or tension problems, it may be time to replace the needle again. It makes a big difference in the assembly of the project when you have a clean machine with a new needle. If you're using a new needle and have tension problems, it's possible the clothesline chosen isn't appropriate. See "Resources" on page 79 for suitable types of clothesline.

Attach an appliqué or zigzag foot to your machine and set the machine for a zigzag stitch that is about ¼" wide. Follow the instructions for the project you're making. When you begin stitching, pull on the bobbin and needle threads to help get the clothesline moving through the machine. To join rows of clothesline, simply lay the wrapped clothesline next to the previous row and zigzag stitch, catching about ⅛" of each row with each stitch. Strive for a uniform zigzag stitch that goes from near the middle of one clothesline to near

To join two lengths of clothesline, overlap ends, glue, and wrap with thread. Wrap with a strip of fabric.

the middle of the clothesline in the adjoining row. If more thread shows than fabric, adjust the spacing of the zigzag stitch.

An oval base is easy to sew. It may be a slower process to stitch the first few rows together at the center of a round base. Zigzag stitch one stitch at a time if necessary, stopping with the needle down, raising the presser foot, and turning the coil slightly before lowering the presser foot and proceeding. After a few stitches, the feed dogs begin to feed the clothesline through the machine. You can also turn the hand wheel to move the presser foot up and down, taking a stitch or two each time, to move the piece through the machine. If bulk is a problem, the feed dogs can be lowered to place the starting piece under the needle. Remember to reengage the feed dogs before starting to sew. If you aren't able to get the wrapped clothesline to move along properly, try using a walking foot.

---

### Zigzag-Stitch and Tension Settings

Before starting your project, make a stitch sample to be sure you have the proper zigzag-stitch setting and the correct tension. Write these settings on a piece of tape and attach it to your machine.

---

Snip any stray threads from the project as you sew or they may become tangled with the zigzag stitches later and look messy. If the wrapped clothesline becomes tangled around the needle area while you're sewing, simply stop stitching with the needle down and twirl that portion of the clothesline free.

Once the base is completed, a piece of tape is adhered to the base to mark the location where all subsequent rows are started and ended, where any changes in fabric or basket shape are made, and where the project is finished off at the end (see "Making Changes" on page 20). Once the base is marked with tape, the sides of the basket are formed. Begin sewing where you left off with the base, following the directions for your project. Each time you reach the tape mark, a row has been added.

Follow the project directions to complete the sides of the basket and finish off at the tape mark, following "Tapering off the Clothesline" on page 24.

You can remove the project from the machine as often as necessary to check the shape. When you're ready to continue, simply insert the project back under the needle and continue where you left off, overlapping the stitching at the new starting point. Each time you change the bobbin, brush out the bobbin case, because these can be very linty projects.

## Making a Round Base

1. Create a tight round coil with the wrapped clothesline, starting at the end and coiling until you have a coil about 1¾" in diameter. It may take several tries. If you have difficulty holding the pieces together, you may want to pin or hand baste the rows in place. Keeping the coil tight (no light should be showing through the center), place it under your presser foot, and straight stitch an X across the coils. This is done to help you zigzag stitch this area without the coil coming apart.

2. Always position the coil under the presser foot so the tail is to the right of the machine needle. Starting at the very center of the coil, zigzag stitch each row of clothesline to the next row using a bamboo stick or stiletto to help hold the clothesline in place. Work your way around each row to the end of the starting coil. An ideal zigzag stitch is ¼" wide (see "Sewing Guidelines" on page 13.)

3. Continue to wrap, coil, and zigzag stitch additional clothesline around the starting coil until the base reaches the size specified in the project instructions. Keep the tail coming through the center area of your machine, to the right of the machine needle, leaving the extra clothesline attached. This is very important! This allows the basket to grow and take shape to the left of the machine where there is ample room. There is not enough room for the basket to be formed to the right of the needle. When your base is finished, remove it from your machine, leaving the extra clothesline attached. Use a piece of tape to mark a point near the edge of the base where fabric or shape changes are to take place (see "Making Changes" on page 20).

## Round Plate

The method used to create the round base for a basket can also be used to make a flat plate or wall hanging. To make a plate like the one shown, follow steps 1 and 2 for "Making a Round Base." Continue to wrap, coil, and zigzag stitch until the project reaches the desired diameter (11½" for a plate). Place a piece of tape on the plate to mark the end of the stitching. Finish the plate, referring to "Tapering Off the Clothesline" on page 24.

## Making an Oval Base

1. To make an oval base, begin with a predetermined length of wrapped clothesline. This will be the baseline. The remaining wrapped clothesline will be coiled around this length. The baseline measurements are listed for the oval projects shown in this book. Mark off the baseline length, fold the clothesline in half at that point, and zigzag stitch the two together at the starting fold with the tail to the right of the needle. An ideal zigzag stitch is ¼" wide (see "Sewing Guidelines" on page 13).

2. Wrap the clothesline around the opposite side of the baseline, turning the corner snugly around the unfilled end of the wrapped clothesline. Zigzag stitch the area using a stiletto or bamboo stick to help hold the clothesline in place. Continue to wrap and zigzag stitch the clothesline around the baseline until the oval base reaches the size specified in the project instructions. Be sure the oval created has straight edges on the long sides. Keep the tail coming through the center area of your machine to the right of the machine needle, leaving the extra clothesline attached. This is very important! This allows the basket to grow and take shape to the left of the machine where there is ample room. When your base is finished, remove it from your machine. Use a piece of tape to mark a point near the edge of the base where changes are to take place (see "Making Changes" on page 20).

Front of project

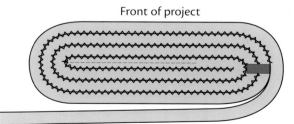

The method used to create an oval base for a basket can also be used to make a flat place mat. To make a place mat like the one shown, follow steps 1 and 2 for "Making an Oval Base" (this place mat started with a baseline measurement of 7¼"). Continue to wrap, coil, and zigzag stitch until a fabric change is desired. Use a piece of tape to mark a point where fabric changes will take place and where the clothesline will be tapered off at the end. Wrap, coil, and zigzag stitch, changing fabrics as desired, until the project reaches the required dimensions (10¼" x 17" for the place mat shown here). Finish the place mat, referring to "Tapering Off the Clothesline" on page 24.

## Making a Square Base

1. Follow the directions in "Making a Round Base" on page 14 to make a round base the size specified in the project instructions. Remove the round base from the machine, leaving the extra clothesline attached.

2. Place the round base on a surface with a grid, such as a cutting mat. Pin the extra wrapped clothesline to the round base, forming a square around it. Use the lines on the grid as a guide for forming the square. The formed square should measure ½" smaller than the square base measurement given in the project directions (it will grow ½" larger when the final row of clothesline is added).

Front of project

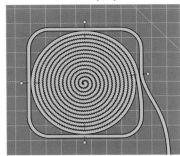

3. Zigzag stitch the four sides of the square to the round base at the center of each side. Use a piece of tape to mark the edge along one side of the base where changes are to take place (see "Making Changes" on page 20). Zigzag stitch a second row of wrapped clothesline around the square, ending your sewing at the tape mark. There should be a gap in the base at each of the corners. Fill the gaps in the base with rows of wrapped clothesline cut to fit.

Front of project

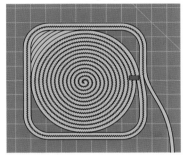

4. Zigzag stitch the wrapped clothesline pieces in place at the corners, stitching one row at a time. A stiletto or bamboo stick will help you hold these pieces of clothesline in place while you zigzag stitch them to an adjoining row.

5. Fill any gaps with pieces of wrapped clothesline and zigzag stitch the clothesline pieces in place. Once you have finished the base, remove it from the machine, leaving the extra clothesline attached.

## Making a Triangular Base

1. Follow the directions in "Making a Round Base" on page 14 to make a round base of the size specified in the project instructions. Remove the round base from the machine, leaving the extra clothesline attached.

2. Place the round base on a surface with a grid, such as a cutting mat. Pin the extra wrapped clothesline to the round base, forming a triangle around it. Use the lines on the grid as an aid for forming the triangle. The size of the triangle base is measured from a corner to the center of the opposite side. Measure from all three corners to be sure the triangle measurements are equal. The formed triangle should measure ½" smaller than the triangle base measurement given in the project directions (it will grow ½" larger when the final row of clothesline is added).

Front of project

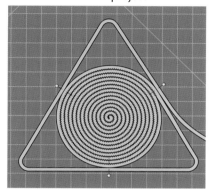

3. Zigzag stitch the three sides of the triangle to the round base at the center of each side. Use a piece of tape to mark the edge along one side of the base where changes are to take place (see "Making Changes" on page 20). Zigzag stitch a second row of wrapped clothesline around the triangle, ending your sewing at the tape mark. There should be a gap in the base at each of the corners. Fill the gaps in the base with rows of wrapped clothesline cut to fit.

Front of project

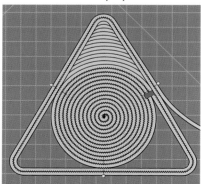

4. Zigzag stitch the wrapped clothesline pieces in place at the corners, stitching one row at a time. A stiletto or bamboo stick will help hold these pieces of clothesline in place while you zigzag stitch them to an adjoining row.

5. Fill any gaps with pieces of wrapped clothesline; glue and zigzag stitch the clothesline pieces in place. Once you have finished the base, remove it from the machine, leaving the extra clothesline attached.

## Making a Figure-Eight-Shaped Base

1. Follow the instructions in "Making a Round Base" on page 14 to make a round base the size specified in the project instructions. Cut off the extra wrapped clothesline. Stitch a second round base with the same diameter, but leave the extra wrapped clothesline attached. Measure the size of the two round base pieces through the center in several locations to be sure the two bases match in size.

2. Place the two base pieces together as shown, positioning the base with the attached clothesline at the top and hiding the cut edge of the remaining base inside the middle join. Join the coils with a zigzag stitch and secure by backstitching. Remove the joined base pieces from the machine and cut any threads. Use a piece of tape to mark where the stitching ended and the clothesline is still attached and label as the front of the project. Place another tape marker on the short side of the figure-eight base furthest from where the stitching ended to mark a point where changes are to take place.

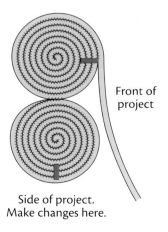

Front of project

Side of project.
Make changes here.

3. Starting where you left off, continue stitching the wrapped clothesline around the new figure-eight-shaped base until you reach the indent where the round bases are joined. Using a stiletto or bamboo stick, push the wrapped clothesline into the indented area tightly to maintain the shape. Any gap will be filled in with wrapped clothesline later. Continue stitching around to the opposite side, and again push the wrapped clothesline into the indented area tightly. Continue to stitch wrapped clothesline around the base, stitching around the front of the project one more time and ending at the side where you placed the tape marker for changes.

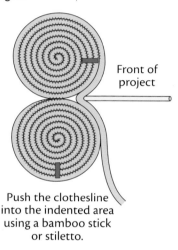

Front of project

Push the clothesline into the indented area using a bamboo stick or stiletto.

## Maintaining the Figure-Eight Shape

Use a ball-headed pin as a marker at the center of the indented sides to know exactly where the indent is.

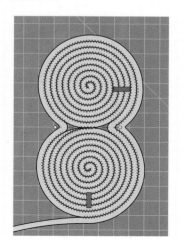

## Making a U-Shaped Heart Base

1. To make a heart-shaped base, begin with a predetermined length of wrapped clothesline. This will be the baseline. The remaining wrapped clothesline will be coiled around this length. The baseline measurements are listed for the heart projects in the book. Mark off the baseline length, fold the clothesline in half at that point, and zigzag stitch the two lines together, starting at the fold (see illustration in step 1 of "Making an Oval Base" on page 15).

2. Wrap the clothesline around the opposite side of the baseline, turning the corner snugly around the unfilled end of the wrapped clothesline. Shape the baseline into a slightly expanded U shape. The distance across the top of the U shape should be about 3" or the measurement listed in the project instructions. Zigzag stitch using a stiletto or bamboo stick to help hold the clothesline in place. Use a piece of tape to mark the center of the U.

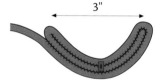

3"

3. Continue to wrap and zigzag stitch the clothesline around the baseline. Push in the rows of clothesline with a stiletto or bamboo stick each time you reach the tape mark at the center to help shape the top of the heart. Keep the tail coming through the center area of your machine to the right of the machine needle, leaving the extra clothesline attached. This is very important! This allows the basket to grow and take shape to the left of the machine where there is ample room. To make a heart with a rounded U-shaped base, continue to wrap and zigzag stitch the clothesline around the baseline until the heart base reaches the size specified in the project instructions. End the stitching on the left side of the heart at its widest measurement across. Remove the heart base from the machine, leaving the extra clothesline attached. Mark the base at the end of the stitching with a piece of tape (see "Making Changes" on page 20).

BASIC TECHNIQUES

## Making a V-Shaped Heart Base

1. Follow steps 1–3 of "Making a U-Shaped Heart Base" on page 18, but stop stitching on the right side of the heart where the heart reaches its widest measurement across and is about 1" smaller than the desired finished width.

2. To form the V shape at the bottom of the heart base, take the base to a surface with a grid, such as a cutting mat. Pin the extra wrapped clothesline around the base, creating a V at the bottom of the heart as shown. Use the lines on the grid as a guide. The measurement of the heart from the center indent at the top to the bottom of the V should be about 1" smaller than the desired finished length. Start stitching where you left off and continue to the gap at the bottom. Break stitching and restart on the left side, stitching wrapped clothesline around the heart until you reach the starting point on the opposite side. Use a piece of tape to mark the edge along the left side of the base where changes are to take place (see "Making Changes" on page 20).

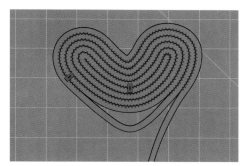

Front of project

3. Zigzag stitch a second row of clothesline around the bottom of the heart. End your sewing at the tape mark. There should be a gap in the base at the bottom of the heart. Fill the gap in the base with rows of wrapped clothesline cut to fit.

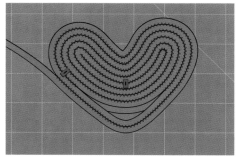

Front of project

4. Zigzag stitch the wrapped clothesline pieces in place at the lower portion of the V, stitching one row at a time. A stiletto or bamboo stick will help you hold these pieces of clothesline in place while you zigzag stitch them to an adjoining row. Once you have finished the base, remove it from the machine, leaving the extra clothesline attached.

## ADDING A LABEL

When the base for a project other than a purse or plate is completed, it's time to add a label to the underside. Do it now, because once the project is completed, it may be difficult to fit it under the presser foot to sew on the label. I stitch labels to the inside of purses when the project is nearly complete. I glue labels to the back of plates when complete, following the same procedure as for a basket or bowl but using hand stitching in place of machine stitching. For a basket or bowl, choose a side of the base to be the front of the project and, with the front away from you, flip the base over to the other side. Glue the label to the center of the base so that the tag is parallel to the front of the project. Straight stitch completely around the edges of the label. Remove the base from the machine, trim the thread tails, and flip it back over to the right side. The label stitching will be visible on the top side of the project, so use matching thread. Don't cut the wrapped clothesline when you add the label; you will continue wrapping the clothesline around the base to form the sides.

Front of project

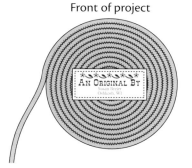

Label stitched to the bottom
of a round base coil

You can use a purchased label or you can make a label by writing the pertinent information on a small piece of fabric with a Pigma pen. If you're writing your own message, heat set the ink with an iron before attaching the label to the project.

## MAKING CHANGES

Always mark the base with a piece of tape at the location where changes are to take place. You may want to draw an arrow on the tape mark using a permanent marker. The tape mark, or arrow, is the point where rows are started and ended and where your project will change angle positions to achieve the desired shaping. This is also the point where you can change to a contrasting fabric and where the project will be finished off. As the project grows and the sides of the basket get taller, it may become difficult to easily see the tape mark. You may want to add a second tape mark, in line with the first one, on the inside edge of the basket so it can be seen as new rows are added. To make any fabric changes and tapering off at the end of a project less noticeable, follow these guidelines:

- If you plan to add handles to your project, use the side of the project as the point of change. The handles will hide the transitions. I use the right side of the project (left side for a heart basket) so the end of the clothesline will be near the back of the project when the project is finished off.

- If you aren't adding handles, use the back of the project, close to the sides, where changes will be less noticeable.

- If there will be a large embellishment on the front to cover it, make changes at the front of the project.

## CHANGING FABRICS

Always use a piece of tape to mark the base where changes are to take place. To make a fabric change in a project that isn't a scrappy project, stitch until you come to the tape mark, trim off the remainder of the fabric strip you're working with, glue the end in place, and secure with a pin. Glue and wrap the new strip of fabric around the same piece of clothesline slightly overlapping the previous wrapped fabric and continue stitching. It may be necessary to change the thread on the machine to match the new fabric.

Front of project

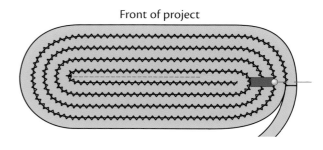

If you're using different fabrics for the base and the side of a project, sew one row of your side fabric as the last row on your base. Doing this prevents the base fabric from peeking through at the sides.

## BUILDING UP THE SIDES OF THE PROJECT

To build up the sides of the project, sew additional rows of clothesline to the base while holding the base in one of four basic angle positions to achieve the desired shaping. The angle-position samples (shown on pages 21–24) are stitched with contrasting thread for clarity. Angle positions 1 and 2 are typically sewn for just one row each, to transition from the base to the side of the project. Angle position 3 is used for the sides of the project and produces a project with sides that angle out slightly. Angle position 3 also has three variations. The first variation produces a project with sharply angled sides and resembles a V shape. The second variation uses a fingertip lift, which produces straight sides on large projects and produces nearly straight sides on small projects. The third variation is for large projects and produces sides that taper in at the rim. Remember that not all machines will produce exactly the same result because each machine is different. The distance the needle is from the side edge of the machine influences how the basket takes its shape. Built-in cabinet machines might be limited when stitching in angle position 4, which is most often used as an optional step for creating a rolled upper edge on a project. Follow the instructions for your project to determine which of these angles to use and in what order.

## Angle Position 1

This angle position creates a gradual transition from the base to the sides. Use this angle to begin shaping a curved outer edge on a flat base. Place the base under the presser foot at the location of the tape marker. Place your left index fingertip under the outer row of the base. Lift up slightly. The positioning of your fingertip underneath as you sew will produce the correct amount of curve around the outer edge of the piece. Stitch one row around the base, holding your hand position the same until you return to the tape mark, and then stop with the needle down. The row just stitched should be raised slightly above the base. Begin and end each row at the tape mark.

## Angle Position 2

This angle position creates a sharper transition from the base to the sides. Use this angle to gradually build the curve in the basket where the clothesline rises up from the base. With the base under the presser foot, lift the base up midway between the bed of the machine and the flat vertical side edge of the machine. Starting at the tape mark, stitch one row around the project, holding your hand position the same until you return to the tape mark, and then stop with the needle down.

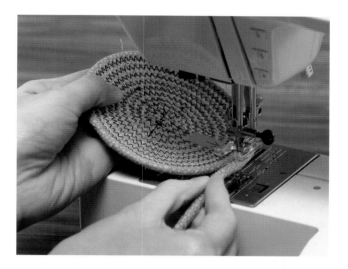

## Angle Position 3

This angle position creates a basket with slightly angled sides. Use this angle to complete the curve in the basket where the clothesline rises up from the base and continue in this position to complete a basket with slightly angled sides. With the project under the presser foot, lift the base with your left hand until it touches the vertical side of the sewing machine (see top photo on page 22). Starting at the tape mark, stitch one row around the project, holding the same hand position and continuing past the tape mark to complete the transition from flat base to side. For a project with slightly angled sides, continue stitching rows around the project in this position until the project reaches the desired height. Stop stitching 2" before you reach the tape mark on the last row and follow the project instructions to finish the project.

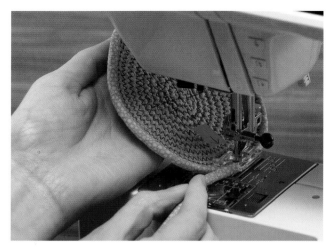

Begin sewing in angle position 3 with the base touching the vertical side of the machine.

As the project grows in angle position 3, it should continue to touch the vertical side of the machine as rows are added.

Angle position 3 has three additional variations. Use variation 1 to produce a basket with more angled sides (see the V-shaped basket at right), use variation 2 to produce a basket with less angled sides (see the straight-sided basket on page 23), and use variation 3 to produce a basket with tapered sides near the rim (see the tapered basket on page 23).

## Angle Position 3, Variation 1 (V-Shaped Basket)

In order to make this basket, your machine bed must be level with the surrounding work surface to prevent distorting the basket. An acrylic extension table is ideal.

With the project under the presser foot, lift the base with your left hand until it touches the vertical side of the sewing machine as shown in the top photo, left. Starting at the tape mark, stitch one row around the project, holding the same hand position and continuing past the tape mark to complete the transition from flat base to side. Continue stitching rows around the base in the same manner until you feel the machine bed taking over the shaping of the basket. It sounds strange, but it does happen! If you let the machine bed or the work surface guide the project, you will get a wider opening and the sides of the basket will angle out sharply. Continue stitching rows of clothesline around the basket, letting the machine bed do the shaping, until the side of the basket reaches the desired height. Stop stitching 2" before you reach the tape mark on the last row and follow the project instructions to finish the project.

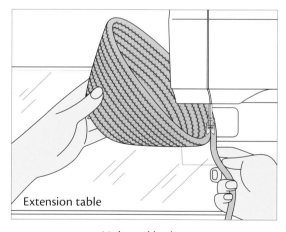

Extension table

V-shaped basket

## Angle Position 3, Variation 2 (Straight-Sided Basket)

For projects with high sides, it's best to have the machine bed level with the surrounding work surface to prevent distorting the basket. This variation works particularly well on projects that are large enough to clear the top of the machine as rows are being

BASIC TECHNIQUES

added. With the project under the presser foot, lift the base with your left hand until the coil touches the vertical side of the sewing machine as shown in the top photo, opposite. Starting at the tape mark, stitch one row around the project, holding the same hand position and continuing past the tape mark to complete the transition from flat base to side. Continue stitching rows around the base in the same manner; as soon as it becomes possible, wedge the fingertips of your left hand under the project. As the project becomes larger, insert your fingertips further under the side of the project, but only as far as the first knuckle. This slight fingertip lift will produce a basket with a straighter side. For large baskets that encircle the side edge of the sewing machine, keep the basket base parallel to the side edge of the machine as the basket grows. Regularly take the basket out from the machine and examine it to see how the sides are shaping up and make any needed adjustments. Continue stitching rows of clothesline around the basket until the sides of the basket reach the desired height. Stop stitching 2" before you reach the tape mark on the last row and follow the project instructions to finish the project.

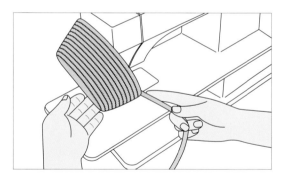

Small straight-sided basket

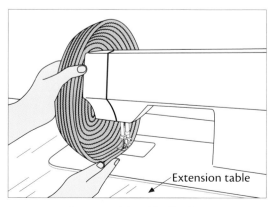

Large straight-sided basket

## Angle Position 3, Variation 3 (Tapered Basket)

Use this variation on projects that are large enough to clear the top of the machine as rows are being added. It works well for tapering in the sides of large round baskets or to taper in the short sides on large oval or figure-eight baskets.

With the project under the presser foot, lift the base with your left hand until it touches the vertical side of the sewing machine as shown in the top photo, opposite. Starting at the tape mark, stitch one row around the project, holding the same hand position and continuing past the tape mark to complete the transition from flat base to side. Continue stitching rows around the base in the same manner to produce straight sides, until tapering is desired. At that point stop at the tape mark with the needle down. Tilt the basket to the right over the top of the machine using your left hand to lift up the base of the basket. Continue stitching rows around the base until the sides of the basket reach the desired height. Stop stitching 2" before you reach the tape mark on the last row and follow the project instructions to finish the project.

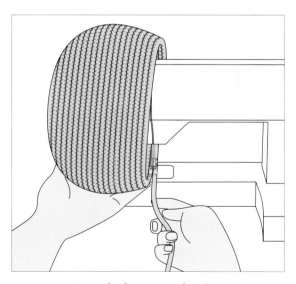

Large basket, tapered at rim

## Angle Position 4 (Rolled Edge)

This angle is used to build a rolled outer edge on a basket after the desired height has been achieved. Remove any extension tables from your machine. Place the project under the presser foot at the tape mark with the edge of the project on the arm of the sewing machine. Push the remainder of the project lower than the machine bed at the side edge. Zigzag stitch around the project for the number of rows indicated in the project instructions (usually three to five), stopping 2" before you reach the tape mark on the last row; follow the project instructions to finish the project. Use your hands to roll the top edge of the basket over.

Create a rolled edge by pushing the project down, lower than the machine bed for the last few rows. This photo shows the project near completion. Usually the edge does not roll over on its own. Use your hands to shape the rollover.

When adding rows of wrapped clothesline to the sides of some basket shapes, you may notice the sides beginning to dip down. If you notice a dip in the sides of the basket as it's being constructed, use one of the following methods to correct the problem.

- Use a bamboo stick to push the ends of the basket in while stitching to compact that area a bit. Continue this for several rows until the sides are even with the ends.

- Double wrap the clothesline in the problem area, and then zigzag stitch it into place. Repeat on the next several rows if necessary. This is often the best solution.

- If you notice severe dipping too late and you're using one color of wrapped clothesline, you can still even out the remaining rows. Wrap and sew a short clothesline piece to the problem area for one or more rows to even out the sides.

## TAPERING OFF THE CLOTHESLINE

Unwrap the clothesline and cut it 1¼" past the tape mark. Do not cut the fabric yet. Starting at the tape mark, gradually trim the clothesline along the length at an angle to reduce the bulk, trimming the most near the very end of the clothesline. Apply glue to the wrong side of the fabric strip (not the clothesline), and then wrap the remaining clothesline very tightly until you're wrapping only fabric. Trim off the excess fabric. Hold the remaining tail very snugly to the project using a stiletto or bamboo stick and zigzag stitch it in place. Continue to zigzag stitch over the last row of clothesline along the outer edge of the project until you reach the end. This step helps prevent fraying.  Remove the project from the machine and trim the thread tails.

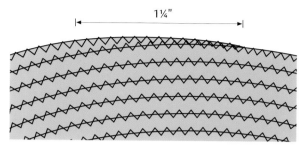

1¼"

Taper the end of the clothesline to blend it into the outer edge of the basket.

## Reshaping a Bumpy Ending

If your tapered clothesline doesn't blend in smoothly with the top edge of the basket and results in a small bump, simply squeeze or finger-press the clothesline at that point while the glue is still wet to compress it and create a smoother transition. Hold the area in place by inserting straight pins from the top straight down through the coils until dry. Do not push the pins in too deeply or that might result in small indentations.

# CORRECTING MISTAKES

Often when you make mistakes on these projects, you don't need to get out the seam ripper! Mistakes are usually easy to correct or camouflage. Here are some suggestions for correcting mistakes.

- If your sewing line strays, go back over it a second time the correct way.

- If you notice a spot of exposed clothesline showing, you can dab some color over it using a matching permanent-ink marker. Or, if the exposed gap is large, simply take a snip of fabric, glue it over the spot, and zigzag stitch over it.

- If you see light through the center of a base, apply glue to a small piece of fabric, wedge it into that area, and stitch in place.

## Preventing Floppy Baskets

Long baskets or very large baskets have the potential to become floppy. Use the guidelines below to prevent or correct floppiness.

- Use a slightly tighter zigzag stitch when constructing the basket.

- Choose a fabric with a high thread count.

- Use fabric glue more often when wrapping the clothesline, but remember to use it lightly.

- Machine stitch a 2½" double binding at the top of the basket for more strength.

- Stitch wrapped clothesline in a decorative pattern around the sides of the basket.

- Use Aleene's or Crafter's Pick fabric stiffener on the basket. To stiffen a basket, I've used a spray bottle to lightly cover it with a mixture of one-half stiffener and one-half water. I then allowed the basket to air-dry on a wire rack. The solution dried clear, left no residue, and stiffened my basket. It's best to start with a light application first. Another coat can be added later, if needed.

# CARE INSTRUCTIONS

When a finished project gets dusty, vacuum it lightly. If it's soiled, spot clean with a little soap and water first. If that doesn't work, hand wash it in cool water with a gentle detergent; rinse thoroughly. Pat with a thirsty towel, and then air-dry after reshaping. Please don't try to machine wash these items because it might fray some of the edges of the fabric strips or damage the embellishments.

Avoid placing your fabric projects in the sunlight because they will fade over time. Also, don't use any fabric softener at any time during the process—it will stop fusibles from bonding and make the project floppy.

BASIC TECHNIQUES

# ROUND BASKETS

Round baskets are versatile and easy to make. Stitching a basket with just one fabric is fastest, but for more interest you can change fabrics to create striped patterns, or choose from numerous embellishing ideas to add to the finished basket.

## Round Striped Basket

Create this striped basket by making a 5½"-diameter round base from red print, but change to yellow print for the last row of the round base. Build up the sides by adding one yellow row in angle position 2 and two more rows in angle position 3 for a total of four yellow rows. Change to red fabric and add nine more rows in variation 2 of angle position 3. Continuing in this position, add four more yellow rows, and then finish off the basket. Make reversed S-coil handles with cabochon accents (see "Wrapped Clothesline Handles" on page 59). The top of the basket measures 8½" across and the basket stands 3½" high.

26

# BASIC ROUND BASKET

### Finished Measurements

Height without embellishments: 2"

Base diameter: 4½"

Diameter across top: 7"

A small scrappy basket is embellished along the rim with braid trim and multicolored glass beads. Round baskets are the fastest and easiest to sew. This small basket is a good size for a starter project and allows you an opportunity to be creative with embellishments. For ideas, see "Embellishments" on page 63.

## Materials

See "Basic Supplies" on page 8 and "Tools and Equipment" on page 9.

10 yards of clothesline

½ yard or scraps of fabric

¾ yard of flexible black braid trim, ⅝" wide, for embellishing (optional)

Size 6 seed beads for embellishment (optional)

## How to Make a Basic Round Basket

Refer to "Cutting Fabric Strips" on page 11 and "Wrapping Clothesline with Fabric Strips" on page 12 to prepare the wrapped clothesline. Refer to "Basic Techniques" on page 10 for details as needed.

1. Make a round base that's 4½" in diameter.

2. Add a label to the underside of the base, if desired.

3. Build up the sides around the base by stitching one row around the coil in angle position 1. Then stitch one row around the coil in angle position 2. Change to angle position 3 and stitch rows around the project until the sides measure 2" high. Stop stitching 2" before you reach the tape mark on the last row.

4. Taper off the clothesline to finish the basket.

5. Add embellishments to the basket, if desired (see "Embellishments" on page 63). This basket has decorative braid trim folded over the rim and glued and stitched in place. Multicolored glass size 6 seed beads are stitched on top of the braid trim (see "Beads and Buttons" on page 64).

# OVAL BASKETS

The difference in the shape of a round basket and an oval basket is determined at the starting point. For a round basket, you coil the wrapped clothesline around itself in a circular manner; for an oval basket, you coil the wrapped clothesline around a predetermined straight length of wrapped clothesline (referred to as the baseline). For a small basket, start with a baseline that measures about 3" and for a medium-sized basket, start with a baseline of about 4½". Either of these sizes would be good for a first project. Larger baskets, such as long bread baskets, have a tendency to become floppy. To prevent this, follow the tips in "Preventing Floppy Baskets" on page 25.

### Oval Basket with Coiled Handles

To construct this basket, make a 6½" x 3¾" oval base, starting with a 3" baseline. Build up the sides by stitching all rows in variation 2 of angle position 3. When the basket reaches 1½" high, change to contrasting fabric. Stitch a total of 6 more rows, alternating between the contrasting fabric and the main fabric, finishing with the main fabric. Stop stitching at the side of the basket. Do not cut the clothesline. Make and attach the loosely coiled handles and bead embellishments (see "Wrapped Clothesline Handles" on page 59). The finished basket is 3" tall and the top opening measures 8¾" x 6".

# BASIC OVAL BASKET

Finished Measurements

Height: 4"

Base dimensions: 6" x 2"

Size of top opening: 10" x 6½"

Striped detailing accents the animal print! This medium-sized oval basket is perfect for holding small loose items, such as jewelry, coins, or office supplies. It's a great size to start with if this is your first oval basket. A contrasting stripe was added to the middle of this basket. If you prefer, stitch all the rows using the same fabric. Keep in mind that an oval basket can become an oval purse. If you love the look of the basket and have enough fabric, keep coiling until the basket reaches the desired height for a purse. Refer to "Purses" on page 38 for handle, closure, and pocket ideas.

## Materials

See "Basic Supplies" on page 8 and "Tools and Equipment" on page 9.

15 yards of clothesline

⅝ yard of main fabric

¼ yard of contrasting fabric

## How to Make a Basic Oval Basket

Refer to "Cutting Fabric Strips" on page 11 and "Wrapping Clothesline with Fabric Strips" on page 12 to prepare the wrapped clothesline. Refer to "Basic Techniques" on page 10 for details as needed.

1.  Make a 6" x 2" oval base, starting with a baseline measurement of 4¾".

2.  Add a label to the underside of the base, if desired.

3.  Build up the sides around the base by stitching one row in angle position 1 and one row in angle position 2. Change to angle position 3, stitch seven rows around the project, and then change fabrics (see "Changing Fabrics" on page 20). Check the sides often for dipping. If dipping occurs, follow the tips for "How to Correct Dipping Sides" on page 24.

4.  Continuing in angle position 3, stitch three rows around the project using clothesline wrapped with a contrasting fabric, and then change back to the main fabric. Continue in angle position 3, stitching six rows around the project. Stop stitching 2" before you reach the tape mark on the last row.

5.  Taper off the clothesline to finish the basket.

# SQUARE BASKETS

The square basket is a simple variation of the round basket. I start with a round coiled base, and then create a square around it. Use additional wrapped clothesline to fill in the gaps in the corners between the square outline and the round base. Once the square base is complete, you simply build up the sides until the basket reaches the desired height.

## BASIC
## SQUARE BASKET

| Finished Measurements |
| --- |
| Height: 3¼" |
| Square base: 5½" |
| Round base: 4½" |
| Distance across top: 8¼" |

A small square basket is embellished with contrasting double binding and fusible appliqué. Beads and French knots accent the appliqué. If you prefer, you can make the whole basket from the same fabric. See "Embellishments" on page 63 for additional ideas. If you're designing your own square basket, a good size for the starting round base is between 3" and 6" in diameter.

## Materials

See "Basic Supplies" on page 8 and "Tools and Equipment" on page 9.

15 yards of clothesline

½ yard of main fabric

½ yard of contrasting fabric

Scrap of fabric for appliqué (optional)

Scrap of fusible web for appliqué (optional)

Assorted beads for embellishment (optional)

Embroidery floss for embellishment (optional)

## How to Make a Basic Square Basket

Refer to "Cutting Fabric Strips" on page 11 and "Wrapping Clothesline with Fabric Strips" on page 12 to prepare the wrapped clothesline. Refer to "Basic Techniques" on page 10 for details as needed.

1.  Using clothesline wrapped with contrasting fabric, make a 5½" square base by first starting with a 4½" round base.

2.  Add a label to the underside of the base, if desired.

3.  Starting at the tape mark, wrap the clothesline with the main fabric (see "Changing Fabrics" on page 20). With the base in a flat position, zigzag stitch a row of clothesline wrapped with the main fabric around the square. Adding this row of clothesline that's wrapped with the main fabric to the base ensures that the base color won't show at the lower edges of the sides.

4.  Build up the sides around the base by stitching one row around the base in angle position 1. Change to angle position 3 and stitch rows around the base for 1". Change to variation 2 of angle position 3 and continue until the basket reaches 3¼" high. Stop stitching 2" before you reach the tape mark on the last row.

5.  Taper off the clothesline to finish the basket.

6.  Add a 2" to 2½" double binding to the basket, if desired, using contrasting fabric (see "Double Binding" on page 68). Cut a design from a patterned fabric and fuse it to the front of the basket, if desired (see "Fused Appliqué" on page 66). Stitch beads to the appliqué and embroider French knots along the side edges of the appliqué pieces, if desired, to complete the embellishment (see "French Knots" on page 66).

## Square Basket with a Rolled Upper Edge

A square basket edged with narrow satin ribbon and a cluster of small silk flowers makes this batik basket very feminine. Make a 4½" square base by starting with a 3½" round base. Build up the sides by stitching rows in angle position 3 for 1"; then change to variation 2 of angle position 3 and continue until the basket reaches 2¼" high. Create a curved outer edge on the basket by changing to angle position 4 and adding three or four more rows (three rows were used in the basket shown). If necessary, bend the top edge of the basket over and finger-press. Glue narrow satin ribbon around the outer edge of the basket. Embellish the basket with silk flowers (see "Silk Flowers" on page 64). The basket measures 8¼" square at the top, including the rolled edge.

# TRIANGLE BASKETS

A triangle basket starts with a round base, and then a triangle outline of wrapped clothesline is formed around it. Additional wrapped clothesline is used to fill in the gaps in the corners between the triangle outline and the round base.

## Triangle Basket with Corner Handle Grips

Make a 6¼" triangle base by first starting with a 4¼" round base. Build up the sides around the base by stitching one row in angle position 2. Change to variation 2 of angle position 3 and stitch rows until the basket measures 4" high. Periodically stop stitching and use your hands to shape the corners of the triangle. Check the sides often for dipping. If dipping occurs, follow the tips for "How to Correct Dipping Sides" on page 24. When the basket reaches 4" high, stop at the tape mark and remove the basket from the machine. Don't cut the clothesline. Construct the handles and finish the basket following the instructions for "Corner Handle Grips" on page 61. To embellish the basket as shown, refer to "Jeweled Fabric Accents" on page 67. The finished basket measures 4¾" high, including the handle, and 9" across the top from one corner to the opposite side.

# BASIC TRIANGLE BASKET

## Finished Measurements

Height: 2"

Triangle base: 6"

Round base: 4"

Size of top opening from corner
to opposite side: 7½"

This multifunctional basket can be sitting out in plain view or it can be nudged into a corner when space is tight. Whether it's used for keys and pocket change by the doorway or for holding today's lipstick and jewelry on your vanity, it's an unusual shape that works well. This one is decorated with Scribbles paint and earth-tone beads. If you're designing your own triangle basket, a good starting size for the round base would be between 3" and 6" in diameter.

## Materials

See "Basic Supplies" on page 8 and "Tools and Equipment" on page 9.

10 yards of clothesline

½ yard of fabric

Scribbles paint and short-bristle paintbrush for embellishment (optional)

Beads for embellishment (optional)

## How to Make a Basic Triangle Basket

Refer to "Cutting Fabric Strips" on page 11 and "Wrapping Clothesline with Fabric Strips" on page 12 to prepare the wrapped clothesline. Refer to "Basic Techniques" on page 10 for details as needed.

1. Make a 6" triangle base by first starting with a 4" round base.

2. Add a label to the underside of the base, if desired.

3. Build up the sides around the base by stitching one row in angle position 1.

4. Change to variation 2 of angle position 3 and stitch rows around the base until the basket measures 2" high. Periodically stop stitching and use your hands to shape the correct corner angles. Stop stitching 2" before you reach the tape mark on the last row.

5. Taper off the clothesline to finish the basket. Shape the triangle.

6. Using a short bristle brush, paint the upper edge of the basket and a 4½" x ½" solid band on the center of each side, if desired, with Scribbles paint. Use painter's tape to mark off the size of the painted bands. When dry, stitch flat wooden buttons topped with small glass beads onto the painted area using a double length of thread. Further secure the beads with liquid glue.

# Figure-Eight Baskets

The base for the figure-eight basket is constructed by joining two round bases, and then bordering them with a couple of rows of wrapped clothesline. Coiling the wrapped clothesline around the figure-eight base produces a dip in the sides of the basket at the center front and back, giving the upper edge a scalloped appearance.

## Figure-Eight Basket with Satin and Bead Trim

Make a 7½" x 4" figure-eight base, starting with two 3" round bases. Add two more rows around the base to increase the size to 8½" x 5". Build up the sides around the base by adding one row in angle position 2 and the remaining rows in angle position 3 until the basket reaches 3¼" high. Green satin ribbon with a picot edge was glued across the rim of the basket and matching size 11 seed beads were stitched just above the picot edging on both the interior and exterior using a double strand of thread. The finished basket measures 10" x 6½" across the top.

# BASIC FIGURE-EIGHT BASKET

| Finished Measurements |
| --- |
| Height: 4½" |
| Figure-eight base: 8" x 4½" |
| Round bases: 3½" |
| Size of top opening: 10" x 6½" |

This figure-eight basket was constructed from one fabric. Beaded edging defines the rim and accents the center front and back. If you're designing your own figure-eight basket, a good starting size for the round bases would be between 3" and 3½" in diameter. This will produce a medium-sized basket.

## Materials

See "Basic Supplies" on page 8 and "Tools and Equipment" on page 9.

20 yards of clothesline

1¼ yards of fabric

Seed beads and small round beads for embellishment (optional)

## How to Make a Basic Figure-Eight Basket

Refer to "Cutting Fabric Strips" on page 11 and "Wrapping Clothesline with Fabric Strips" on page 12 to prepare the wrapped clothesline. Refer to "Basic Techniques" on page 10 for details as needed.

1. Make a figure-eight base by first starting with two 3½" round bases (1" smaller than the width of the finished figure-eight base).

2. Add a label to the underside of the base, if desired.

3. Build up the sides around the base by stitching one row in angle position 2; use a stiletto or bamboo stick to push the wrapped clothesline into the indented area tightly to maintain the shape. Change to angle position 3 and continue building the sides of the basket using the stiletto or bamboo stick to push the wrapped clothesline into the indented area. Check each row to be sure the indents of each row align with the indented area at the base of the basket. When possible, change to variation 2 of angle position 3. Allow the sides of the basket to encircle the top of the sewing machine in order to produce straight sides on the basket. Continue until the basket measures 4½" high. Stop stitching 2" before you reach the tape mark on the last row.

4. Taper off the clothesline to finish the basket.

5. Add beads to the rim and center front and back of the basket, if desired. For the design shown, beads were strung in a repeating pattern of five seed beads followed by one slightly larger bead on a double strand of thread, and then positioned across the rim. The strand was then tacked in place after every couple beads. A 1" beaded length was stitched to the center front and back, alternating seed beads with the larger beads.

# Heart Baskets

There are two heart-shaped bases to choose from for heart baskets. One creates a heart that has a rounded bottom (U shaped) and one has a sharper point at the bottom (V shaped). To make your own heart design, create the base style of your choice, referring to the appropriate directions on page 18 or 19, and build the basket sides following steps 3 and 4, opposite.

## Scrappy U-Shaped Heart Basket

Make an 8" x 4" heart base, starting with a baseline measurement of 6" and using the instructions for "Making a U-Shaped Heart Base" on page 18; the measurement between the ends of the starting U shape should be 4½". Build up the sides around the base by stitching one row in angle position 2. Change to angle position 3 and stitch three rows. Change to variation 2 of angle position 3 and continue until the basket measures 2" high. The basket measures 9¼" across x 6¼" long at the center top.

*V-Shaped Heart Basket*

# V-SHAPED HEART BASKET

| Finished Measurements |
| --- |
| Height: 2" |
| Width: 7¼" |
| Length at center: 6" |

The splash of metallic gold in the red print fabric gives this basket visual interest without the need for further embellishments. A heart-shaped basket is perfect for anyone that holds a special place in your life. Fill it with goodies, wrap it with plastic wrap, and tie with a ribbon to turn it into a gift basket. To make your own heart design, create the base style of your choice, referring to the appropriate directions on page 18 or 19. Build the basket sides following steps 3 and 4, opposite.

## Materials

See "Basic Supplies" on page 8 and "Tools and Equipment" on page 9.

10 yards of clothesline

½ yard of fabric

## How to Make a V-Shaped Heart Basket

Refer to "Cutting Fabric Strips" on page 11 and "Wrapping Clothesline with Fabric Strips" on page 12 to prepare the wrapped clothesline. Refer to "Basic Techniques" on page 10 for details as needed.

1. Make a 5¼" x 3" heart base, starting with a baseline measurement of 5" and using the instructions for "Making a V-Shaped Heart Base" on page 19; the measurement between the ends of the starting U shape should be 3½".

2. Add a label to the underside of the base, if desired.

3. Build up the sides around the base by stitching one row in angle position 2. Change to angle position 3 and stitch three rows. Change to variation 2 of angle position 3 and stitch four rows around the project. The project should measure 2" high. Stop stitching 2" before you reach the tape mark on the last row.

4. Taper off the clothesline to finish the basket. Reshape the basket if necessary.

# PURSES

The wrapping and coiling method used for making baskets is suitable for purses as well. The basic oval purse is essentially a narrow oval basket with taller sides, plus handles, a closure, and pockets. A second purse style that I've created with wrapped clothesline is the vertical wrapped-clothesline purse. For this style the wrapped clothesline is cut to predetermined lengths, stitched to a base fabric, and then sewn into a purse.

## BASIC OVAL PURSE

| Finished Measurements |
| --- |
| Height without handles: 8" |
| Height with handles: 13" |
| Width across top: 14" |

The basic purse shape is created in the same way as an oval basket (see page 28). Following are the basic steps for constructing a purse with purchased handles, pockets, and a Velcro closure.

## Materials

See "Basic Supplies" on page 8 and "Tools and Equipment" on page 9.

36 yards of clothesline

1¾ yards total of fabric (use 6 different fabrics: fabrics A, B, C, D, E, and F)

¼ yard of fusible interfacing

⅛ yard of fusible web

Purse handles

Velcro

## How to Make a Basic Oval Purse

Refer to "Cutting Fabric Strips" on page 11 and "Wrapping Clothesline with Fabric Strips" on page 12 to prepare the wrapped clothesline. Refer to "Basic Techniques" on page 10 for details as needed.

1. Using fabric A, make a 7¾" x 3¾" oval base, starting with a baseline measurement of 4½". Reinforce the finished base with a grid of straight stitches before continuing with the sides.

2. Build up the sides by stitching one row around the base in angle position 1, followed by one row in angle position 2, and then one row in angle position 3. When building up the sides, reinforce the stitching every 8" to 10" by zigzag stitching in reverse for a couple stitches. Change to angle position 3, variation 2, and stitch three more rows around the base, ending at the tape mark. A total of six rows of fabric A should be visible above the base.

3. Change to fabric B (see "Changing Fabrics" on page 20) and stitch six rows around the purse. Change to fabric C and continue to stitch rows around the purse, changing fabrics after every six rows, until all of the remaining fabrics are used.

4. Taper off the clothesline to finish the purse.

5. Make and attach pockets to the interior, if desired (see "Pockets" at right). Then hand or machine stitch a label to the inside.

6. Apply a 2" to 2½" double binding to the top edge of the purse, if desired (see "Double Binding" on page 68).

7. Add purchased handles and a flap with a Velcro closure to the purse as desired (see "Adding Purchased Handles" on page 40 and "Flaps with Velcro Closures" on page 41).

# POCKETS

You will need to determine the finished size of your pocket, based on the finished size of your purse and your personal preferences. I like to attach a large pocket to both the inside front and back of the purse. Position pockets away from the top purse edge so handles, binding, and embellishments can be attached easily. The pocket design used here has a decorative tucked design at the center to create room for carrying bulky items. Pockets must be cut on the straight of grain.

1. Determine the desired size of the finished pocket, keeping in mind that the pocket should be placed about 2" from the top edge of the purse to clear the handles. Add 3" to the desired width of the pocket to allow for 2" taken up in tucks, plus two ½" seam allowances. Add 1" to the desired length to allow for two ½" seam allowances. Cut two pocket pieces from fabric for each pocket.

2. Pin the pocket pieces right sides together and stitch ½" from the edges, leaving an opening on one side for turning. Trim the corners and turn right side out, pushing out the corners. Press the pocket piece, turning in the raw edges along the opening. Edgestitch along all edges.

3. Using a chalk pencil and ruler, mark a line at the center of the pocket, from top to bottom on the wrong side. Draw a fold line from top to bottom, 1" from each side of the center line.

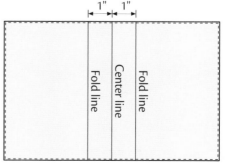

Wrong side of pocket

4. Fold the pocket piece on the outer marked lines and bring the folds to meet the center line. Press. Turn the pocket to the right side. Fold the pocket, wrong sides together, along one of the pressed folds and edgestitch along the fold. Repeat for the remaining pressed fold. Refold the tucks; edgestitch along the upper and lower edges of the tucks to hold them in place. Topstitch 1/4" in from the upper and lower edges.

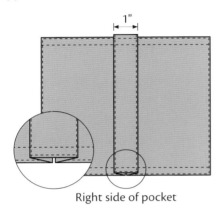

Right side of pocket

5. Pin the pocket to the inside of the purse. Hand stitch or glue in place.

## ADDING PURCHASED HANDLES

Purse handles are available in many sizes and shapes from craft, sewing, or quilting stores. The following steps explain one method for attaching purchased handles to your purse.

1. Cut four pieces of 5"-long clothesline, wrap them with fabric, and zigzag stitch along the length of each piece to secure.

2. Align a handle at the center of the purse along the upper edges. Use pins to mark the handle placement on both sides of the purse front and back. Be certain to measure and mark carefully so that the handles will fit together evenly when the bag is closed.

3. Insert a strip of clothesline through each opening at the base of the handle, from back to front. Wrap the clothesline around and insert through the opening again. Bring the ends together and hold in place with a pin.

4. Cut four 1 1/2" squares from fabric. Press 3/8" to the wrong side on one edge of each square. Place the ends of one of the clothesline strips on the wrong side of a fabric square, over the pressed edge. Stitch the pieces together, stitching four rows spaced a scant 1/4" apart as shown. Repeat at the ends of each handle.

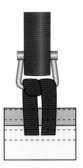

5. Fold 3/8" up at the bottom of a fabric square and fold in the sides to neatly cover the ends of the clothesline pieces. Glue in place. Repeat at the ends of each handle.

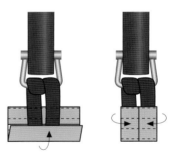

6. Position a handle on one side of the purse and pin the fabric-covered ends of the clothesline to the inside of the purse at the pin mark, placing the end the desired distance down from the upper edge of the purse (about 1 1/4"). Repeat for the other handle.

7. Hold the purse up to check that the handles line up correctly; make any necessary adjustments. Securely hand stitch the fabric squares at the ends of the handles to the inside of the purse. Machine stitch the clothesline at the base of the handles to the inside of the purse, just under the binding at the upper edge.

# FLAPS WITH VELCRO CLOSURES

Velcro closures are a wonderful choice for a purse; if available, purchase Snag-Free Velcro. It comes in several colors, so match it to your fabric as closely as possible. The flap measurements given below are for a flap that fits between a handle with an inner width of 5¼". If your handle width is different, adjust the width of the flap accordingly, allowing for the inner width of the handle plus an extra ½" for two ¼" seam allowances.

1. Cut two 5¾" x 6¼" rectangles from the main flap fabric and one rectangle from lightweight fusible interfacing that is ¼" smaller all around. Center and fuse the rectangle of interfacing to the wrong side of one of the fabric rectangles, following the manufacturer's directions.

2. Place the fabric rectangles right sides together and stitch ¼" from the raw edges on one short edge and the two long edges. Trim the corners and turn right side out, pushing out the corners. Press. Edgestitch along the three stitched edges of the rectangle and baste across the remaining (back) edge to create the purse flap.

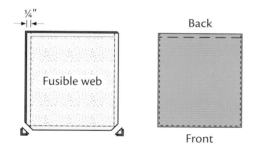

3. Cut one 4¼" x 5½" rectangle from contrasting flap fabric. Cut one 2" x 5½" rectangle from the main flap fabric. For each rectangle, press ¼" to the wrong side on one short edge and the two long edges.

4. Center the main flap fabric rectangle over the contrasting flap fabric rectangle, aligning the pressed edges on the short ends. Stitch the main flap fabric rectangle in place to create the flap accent.

5. Cut a 4" x 5¼" rectangle from fusible web. Fuse the rectangle to the back of the flap accent piece, over the pressed seam allowances, allowing ⅛" of fabric around the edges of the fusible web and following the manufacturer's directions.

6. Center the flap accent piece over the right side of the purse flap, aligning the raw edges. Fuse the accent piece to the purse flap. Edgestitch on the pressed edges of the flap accent piece and baste along the raw edge.

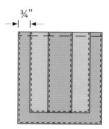

7. Zigzag stitch along the raw edge of the flap. Pin the raw edge of the flap to the inside back of the purse, between the handle ends, ½" below the lower edge of the binding. Bring the purse handles together and check that the flap is in the correct position. Then machine stitch the flap in place on the outside of the purse, along the lower edge of the binding, through all layers. Zigzag stitch the lower edge of the back flap in place.

8. Cut Velcro to size and position one piece of the Velcro on the underside of the flap and stitch in place. Close the flap and mark the position for the corresponding piece of Velcro on the purse front. Stitch the corresponding piece of Velcro in place.

## VERTICAL WRAPPED-CLOTHESLINE PURSE

| Finished Measurements |
| --- |
| Height: 10" |
| Width: 9" |
| Depth: ¾" |

Wrap this purse in your free time away from your sewing machine. Rather than using one continuous piece of wrapped clothesline, the purse is created using precut clothesline and fabric strips. This method allows you to wrap each of the individual clothesline pieces separately at your convenience and join them to a base fabric later. The wrapped lines are less likely to become entangled or to unravel because of the shorter lengths. I chose to use a dark-colored fabric for the purse sides, binding, handles, flap accent, and parts of the main purse panel. I used a medium-colored fabric for the base fabric (lining), main flap, and parts of the main purse panel. A light accent fabric with painted details was used to create four contrasting stripes on the main purse panel. Choose a lining fabric that looks equally nice on both sides, since the wrong side may show between the rows of clothesline. Batik fabric works well.

The purse handles were created from webbing and are inserted through grommets for a designer look. Be sure to use grommets with a shank long enough to accommodate the thickness of the layers. These may need to be purchased from a hardware store. It's a good idea to practice the installation technique on a scrap piece first.

## Materials

See "Basic Supplies" on page 8 and "Tools and Equipment" on page 9.

25 yards of clothesline

¾ yard of main fabric for wrapped clothesline and handles

¾ yard of contrasting fabric for wrapped clothesline, flap, lining, and pocket

¼ yard of accent fabric for wrapped clothesline

2⅛ yards of 1"-wide polyester webbing for straps

¼ yard of fusible interfacing

4 grommets with long shanks

Two 1⅛"-diameter buttons

¾ yard of #18 nylon cording

Grommet setting tool and hammer

Bias tape maker, ½" wide

## The Main Panel

Refer to "Cutting Fabric Strips" on page 11 and "Wrapping Clothesline with Fabric Strips" on page 12 to prepare the wrapped clothesline. Refer to "Basic Techniques" on page 10 for details as needed.

1. Using a clear grid ruler, draw a 9" x 22" rectangle purse pattern on paper. Add a 1" border to all sides of the pattern. The outer drawn lines mark the size of the base fabric or lining. Draw a vertical center line through the pattern. Cut a rectangle on the lengthwise grain from the lining fabric using the outer marked pattern lines. Using a chalk pencil, draw a vertical center line on the wrong side of the lining fabric. Fold the 1" borders on the two long sides of the lining to the wrong side.

2. Cut 29 lengths of clothesline about 22" long and wrap 15 lengths with the main fabric, 10 lengths with contrasting fabric, and 4 lengths with accent fabric. Pin the wrapped fabric to the clothesline pieces at the ends to hold the fabric in place.

3. Place each piece of wrapped clothesline directly on the pattern, arranging the various fabrics in the desired order. I alternated groupings of five dark-colored pieces and five medium-colored pieces and separated each grouping with a single wrapped piece from the accent fabric. No stitching is done at this time.

4. When the entire pattern is covered with wrapped clothesline it's time to sew. Transfer the center piece of wrapped clothesline to the center line on the wrong side of the lining fabric and zigzag stitch down the center of the wrapped clothesline (the accent fabric pieces were straight stitched on both sides instead). Transfer the remaining pieces in the same way, alternating placement on each side of the center. Position the pieces of wrapped clothesline close together to prevent gaps. The rows of clothesline are stitched to the lining separately for this project, rather than joining the rows with zigzag stitching, although you can join the rows with zigzag stitching if you prefer.

When you are close to stitching on the 1" folded area of the lining, make any needed adjustments so full lengths of clothesline will finish off the sides. Move the fold line if necessary.

Center piece

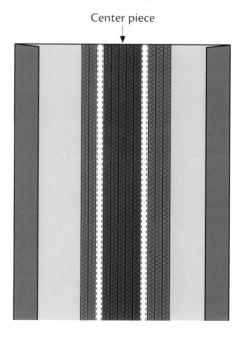

5. Trim the purse panel to 20½", trimming away about ¾" from the top and bottom of the panel to straighten the edges. Straight stitch a reinforcement line ⅛" away from the trimmed areas. Zigzag stitch along the long edges to make the edges stronger.

6. Fold the purse panel in half, matching the cut edges to find the center bottom of the purse. Mark the center of each side with a pin. Reinforce the bottom of the purse with three rows of straight stitches, stitching one row at the center bottom and a row ⅛" out to each side; backstitch often for additional reinforcement.

7. Install grommets following the manufacturer's instructions, but install them so the flattest side of the grommet will be on the lining side. This will prevent the grommet from interfering with the feed dogs during the remaining construction of the purse. Position the grommets so the outside of the grommet will be at least 1" from the short edges of the purse panel and at least one clothesline width from the long edges of the purse panel. The hole on this purse was centered on the third clothesline piece in from the long side edges. Edgestitch around the grommets for reinforcement.

8. If desired, add one or two pockets to the lining side of the purse (see "Pockets" on page 39).

## The Oval Side Panels

Refer to "Cutting Fabric Strips" on page 11 and "Wrapping Clothesline with Fabric Strips" on page 12 to prepare the wrapped clothesline for this project. Refer to "Basic Techniques" on page 10 for details as needed.

1. Make two oval bases, starting with a baseline measurement of 10" and coiling the wrapped clothesline for a total of three rows. The oval bases should measure about 11½" x ¾". End the coiling at one short end of the oval, trim the excess clothesline and fabric a few inches from the end of the stitching.

2. Zigzag stitch around the outer edges of both ovals to make the edges stronger.

3. Pin one oval side panel to the main purse body as shown, aligning the center of the oval with the center stitching line on the main purse body. The oval side piece can be pinned so it's flush with the edges of the main panel or it can be pinned ⅛" toward the inside. Be sure the top cut edges of the purse panel are in alignment. Repeat for the second oval side piece.

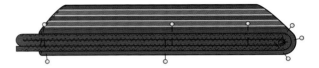

4. Begin securing short sections of one oval side piece to the main purse body with liquid fabric glue, removing pins as necessary, and then repinning until the glue is dry; start at the center bottom of the purse, applying a thin line of liquid glue to the edge of the oval piece. Repeat for the second oval side piece.

5. Hand stitch the oval side pieces in place. Needle-nose pliers will help draw the needle through the bulky areas. To avoid excess threads from showing, push your needle through the wrapped layers rather than on top of them.

6. Let the glue dry, and then remove all straight pins. Place the top of the oval section under the presser foot. Stitch across each oval side panel near the top, aligning the stitching with the stitching lines at the upper edge of the main purse panel front and back to create a continuous line of stitching. After stitching, cut the ends from the oval side panels so the upper edges of the purse are even.

7. Apply double binding to the top edge of the purse (see "Double Binding" on page 68). Cut the binding 2" to 2½" wide, depending on how bulky the fabric is. Use a ¼" seam allowance. Make and attach the shoulder straps (see "Shoulder Straps," opposite). Add a flap with a button closure (see "Flap with Button Closure" on page 45).

# SHOULDER STRAPS

1. Cut two 36" lengths of polyester webbing. Use a ½" bias-tape maker to make two ½" x 36" fabric strips on the straight grain of the fabric. Center the ½"-wide strips over the webbing pieces and edgestitch in place.

2. Cut four 1¼" x 1¾" rectangles of fabric. For each rectangle, fold ⅜" to the wrong side on one of the long edges. Lap the shoulder strap, wrong side up, ⅜" over the folded edge and secure with liquid glue. Wrap the bottom of the rectangle, and then the sides over ⅜". Secure with glue or stitching to cover the end of the shoulder strap.

3. Push the end of one shoulder strap through the grommet hole from the front. Bring it up on the lining side so the end is just under the double binding. Secure in place on the inside and outside with liquid glue where the strap touches the purse. Repeat on the opposite side with the remaining end of the strap, and then attach the second strap to the back of the purse. Hand tack to reinforce.

# FLAP WITH BUTTON CLOSURE

1. Follow steps 1 and 2 on page 41 for "Flaps with Velcro Closures," but cut the two fabric rectangles to 5" x 6¼".

2. Using a ½" bias-tape maker, make a ½" x 11" strip using the straight grain of the fabric. Position the strip ½" from the front edge of the flap front. Wrap the excess to the flap back and turn under the ends at the center back of the flap. Edgestitch the strip in place. This strip will act as a reinforcement for the button.

3. Complete the flap following step 7 of "Flaps with Velcro Closures" on page 41.

4. Cut a 23" length of nylon cording and tie three knots at one end and seven closely spaced knots at the other end. Place the end with the three knots on the center front of the flap over the contrasting strip where the button will cover them. Machine stitch the knotted end of the cording in place.

5. Hand stitch one button over the knots, concealing them. Stitch the other button onto the center front of the purse, about 4" down from the upper edge. Wrap the cording around the buttons in a figure-eight pattern to close the flap.

# LIDS

Lids offer another opportunity to be creative. This chapter includes instructions for making a lid for each basket shape. Some of the lids are flat and some have a raised design. Constructing a lid is similar to making the basket itself. The flat lids start out as the bases of the same shape and similar in size to the basket base. The raised lids start out as miniature baskets and are constructed from the top down. For most basket lids with handles, a small hole is left at the starting point to allow space for attaching the handle.

# MAKING LIDS

Instructions for a round, oval, square, triangle, figure-eight, and heart-shaped lid are provided in this section. You will need to adjust the measurements provided to fit the lid to the basket you have made. When constructing your lid, remove it from the sewing machine often to test fit it on your basket. You may need to sew more or fewer rows in a position than indicated for the lid to fit your specific basket. Use the tips at right to guide you in creating a lid for your basket.

## ROUND BASKET WITH RAISED LID AND LOOPED HANDLE

| Finished Lid Measurements |
| --- |
| Height without handle: 7" |
| Diameter: 12½" |

A batik basket with a raised lid is easy to make when broken down into separately constructed components. The round, domed basket lid with a looped clothesline handle is secured to the matching basket with coiled disks inserted into slits in the lid.

Refer to "Cutting Fabric Strips" on page 11 and "Wrapping Clothesline with Fabric Strips" on page 12 to prepare the wrapped clothesline for the project. Refer to "Basic Techniques" on page 10 and "How to Make a Basic Round Basket" on page 27 as needed.

## Materials (for Both the Basket and Lid)

See "Basic Supplies" on page 8 and "Tools and Equipment" on page 9.

55 yards of clothesline

2 yards of main batik fabric

¼ yard each of two contrasting batik fabrics

⅛"-thick brass ring

## Constructing Successful Lids

- Always sew the basket first, and then make the lid to fit.
- Make the lid a complementary shape and size so that it looks as though it belongs on the basket.
- Plan your handle design first (see "Lid Handles" on page 62) so you know how many clothesline strips or cords will be inserted through the hole at the top. A ¼" to ½" opening is usually enough because you want the handle to fit snugly in the hole. If the hole becomes too large, remedy the problem by adding embellishments around the handle.
- Stitch a small bead to the inside rim of the basket at the center front and on the underside of the lid front. This marks the front of both for a quick matchup.

## How to Make the Round Basket

To make the basket, make a round base that's 8½" in diameter. Build up the sides by adding one row in angle position 2 followed by one row in angle position 3. Change to variation 2 of angle position 3 for three more rows. Change to contrasting fabrics and alternate fabric colors for the next five rows, creating a striped effect, while continuing in variation 2 of angle position 3. Change back to the main batik fabric and continue until the basket measures 4" high; hold your basket straight up over the top of the machine rather than tilting it inward. You want straight sides rather than drawn-in sides. The finished basket is 10¼" in diameter across the top.

## How to Make the Matching Raised Round Lid

1. Using the main batik color, make a round coiled base of three rows of wrapped clothesline, leaving a ½" to ¾" opening at the starting point (¾" was used here) to allow for the handle ends to be pulled to the inside later.

2. Build the sides around the base by stitching 19 rows in variation 1 of angle position 3.

3. Change to contrasting fabric. Changing to angle position 3, alternate contrasting batik fabrics for the next five rows, creating a striped effect to match the basket. Change back to the main batik fabric and variation 2 of angle position 3 and stitch for two more rows.

4. Change to angle position 4 and stitch for eight rows. Check the fit of the lid on the basket. Adjust, if desired, and taper off the lid.

5. To keep the lid securely on the basket, refer to "Keeping Basket Lids Secure: Method 4" on page 57 to add disks to the basket and make slits in the lid.

6. Add a multi-loop wrapped clothesline handle to the lid (see "Lid Handles" on page 62).

## Stabilizing the Basket Rim

To add stability to the rim of a large basket when a large lid is used, add a ⅛"-thick brass ring to the inside rim. If a brass ring in the correct diameter is not available, it's possible to use a slightly smaller-diameter ring and add a strip of batting under the ring to create a snug fit. Whipstitch the ring to the inside of the basket near the rim. Cut a strip of fabric about 1½" wide by the circumference of the basket. Press ¼" of the fabric to the wrong side on each long edge. Straight stitch ⅛" from the edges. Place the fabric strip over the ring, turning under the raw edges at the ends, and use liquid glue and pins to hold it in place. Additionally secure with hand stitching if needed.

# OVAL BASKET WITH RAISED LID

| Finished Lid Measurements |
| --- |
| Height of lid: 2½" |
| Outer dimensions: 8½" x 5¾" |

Basket front

Basket back

Wrapped clothesline basket handles are intertwined with a wrapped clothesline lid decoration, permanently anchoring the lid to the basket. The lid can be hinged open by unfastening a snap on the back side and pulling the clothesline a short distance back through the handle. A dimensional flower on the back of the basket conceals the snap. The basket lid is further embellished with matching dimensional flowers.

Refer to "Cutting Fabric Strips" on page 11 and "Wrapping Clothesline with Fabric Strips on page 12 to prepare the wrapped clothesline for the project. Refer to "Basic Techniques" on page 10 and "How to Make a Basic Oval Basket" on page 29 as needed.

## Materials (for Both the Basket and Lid)

See "Basic Supplies" on page 8 and "Tools and Equipment" on page 9.

25 yards of clothesline

1⅛ yards of fabric for basket

⅛ yard of fabric for dimensional flowers (optional)

HeatnBond Ultra Hold iron-on adhesive for dimensional flowers (optional)

24 small beads (optional)

## How to Make the Oval Basket

To make the basket for the oval lid, make an oval base that's 6" x 3¼", starting with a baseline of 3". Build up the sides by adding one row in angle position 2 and the remaining rows in variation 2 of angle position 3, until the basket measures 2½" high. Taper off the clothesline. The finished basket measures 8¼" x 5¼". Add the handles (see "Wrapped Clothesline Handles" on page 59).

## How to Make the Matching Raised Oval Lid

1. Begin with a 3" baseline. Stitch four rows in angle position 1, and then stitch one row in angle position 2. Change to variation 2 of angle position 3 for ten rows. Return to angle position 1 for three rows. Check to see how the lid is fitting the basket often and make any adjustments. This lid is designed to rest between the side basket handles.

2. Taper off the clothesline to finish the lid.

3. To create the optional wrapped clothesline embellishment that intertwines with the basket handles, first make a 54" length of wrapped clothesline and zigzag stitch down the center. Starting on the right, loop the clothesline across the front of the lid, pinning as you go (see page 49, top photo). Insert one end through the basket handle on the left, and then carry the clothesline straight across the top of the basket and through the remaining basket handle on the right. Determine an end point and pin to the back of the basket. Pin the other end to the side of the basket where desired and trim any excess. Stitch the clothesline in place, letting it hang loose through the handle areas and at the determined end point on the back of the basket. Stitch a snap to the determined end point at the back of the basket and conceal the snap and the other end point with a dimensional fabric flower (see "Dimensional-Fabric Embellishments" on page 65). Add more flowers as desired.

Basket lid

Basket back

# SQUARE BASKET WITH FLAT LID

Finished Lid Measurements

Outer dimensions: 8½" x 8½"

A medium-sized square lid with corner openings sits inside the rim of a square batik basket. The lid features a wooden handle held in place with a piece of knotted wrapped clothesline. A square lid is created in the same way as making a square base for a square basket, except more rows of wrapped clothesline are added to the outer edges. Rather than fill the corners in with wrapped clothesline, I left the gaps at the corners open for added interest. This square basket could act as a good catchall for temporarily storing small items such as lost buttons, an extra key, or a phone number written on a scrap of paper. You may not even have to lift the lid to get the items in the basket. If they are small enough, just slide them through one of the corner openings on top of the lid. If you prefer, fill the openings at the corners with extra pieces of wrapped clothesline in the same way as creating a square base.

Refer to "Cutting Fabric Strips" on page 11 and "Wrapping Clothesline with Fabric Strips" on page 12 to prepare the wrapped clothesline for the project. Refer to "Basic Techniques" on page 10 and "How to Make a Basic Square Basket" on page 31, as needed.

## Materials (for Both the Basket and Lid)

See "Basic Supplies" on page 8 and "Tools and Equipment" on page 9.

36 yards of clothesline

1⅜ yards of fabric

3 wooden wheels, 1" x ⅜"

## How to Make the Square Basket

Make a 7" x 7" square base, starting with a 6" round base. Build up the sides around the base by adding one row in angle position 2. Change to variation 2 of angle position 3 and hold the basket as vertical as possible to achieve straight sides. Continue until the basket measures 5¾" high. Taper off the clothesline and apply a double binding to the upper edge (see "Double Binding" on page 68). Add a lip to the inside of the basket for holding the lid in place (see "Keeping Basket Lids Secure: Method 3" on page 57).

## How to Make the Matching Flat Square Lid

1. Make a 7" square base, starting with a 6" round base; leave a ½" opening at the starting point to allow for the handle ends to be pulled to the inside later (see illustration for step 1 on page 48). Do not fill in the corner gaps with rows of wrapped clothesline. Stitch two or three more rows of wrapped clothesline around the lid as necessary for the lid to fit inside the basket. Check the size often against the basket to make sure it fits. It may be necessary to stitch only a partial row for the last row. That's okay. Taper off when you determine that the lid fits properly.

2. Zigzag stitch around the edges of the corner gaps.

3. Make and attach a handle to the lid (see "Ribbed Wooden Lid Handle" on page 62).

### Setting the Square Shape

Brush fabric stiffener onto the lid and the basket sides, and then pin the lid in place and let dry. This helps the basket and lid hold their square shapes.

# TRIANGLE BASKET WITH RAISED LID

| Finished Lid Measurements |
| --- |
| Height without handle: 3½" |
| Distance from corner to opposite side: 9½" |

Batik fabric can take on a casual or elegant look. I dressed up this triangle lid with beaded drapery tiebacks and head pins strung with beads. Premade bead embellishments can minimize the amount of bead stringing you need to do yourself and cut the time needed for creating the basket embellishments. A triangle lid starts out round, and as the lid grows, it's shaped into a triangle. This gives the lid a flatter surface area at the bottom.

Refer to "Cutting Fabric Strips" on page 11 and "Wrapping Clothesline with Fabric Strips" on page 12 to prepare the wrapped clothesline for the project. Refer to "Basic Techniques" on page 10 and "How to Make a Basic Triangle Basket" on page 33 as needed.

## Materials (for Both the Basket and Lid)

See "Basic Supplies" on page 8 and "Tools and Equipment" on page 9.

29 yards of clothesline

1⅛ yards of fabric

Assorted beads and head pins for embellishment (optional)

2 beaded tassels for embellishment (optional)

## How to Make the Triangle Basket

Make a 6½" triangle base, starting with a 5" round base. Build up the sides around the base by stitching one row in angle position 2 followed by one row in angle position 3. Change to variation 2 of angle position 3 and continue stitching rows until the basket is 3¼" high. Use your hands to define the shape often. Taper off the clothesline. The finished basket across the top measures 8½" from one corner to the center of the opposite side.

## How to Make the Matching Raised Triangle Lid

1. Make a round coiled base of two rows of wrapped clothesline, leaving a ½" opening at the starting point to allow for the handle ends to be pulled to the inside later (see illustration for step 1 on page 48).

2. Build the sides of the lid by stitching one row around the base in angle position 2, and then change to variation 1 of angle position 3 and stitch for 3½". Check your shape often.

3. Take the lid to a surface with a grid, such as a cutting mat. Pin the wrapped clothesline to the base of the lid to form a triangle around the base of the lid.

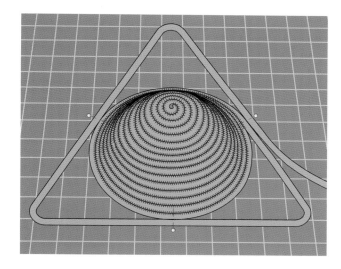

4. Zigzag stitch the three sides of the triangle to the lid base at the center of each side. Zigzag stitch one more row of clothesline around the triangle. There should be a gap in the lid at each of the corners. Fill in the gaps with rows of wrapped clothesline cut to fit and stitch the clothesline in place.

5. Continue stitching rows of clothesline around the triangle lid in angle position 1 until the lid extends beyond the edges of the basket by ½".

6. Taper off the clothesline to finish the lid. Add a lip to the inside of the lid for holding the lid in place (see "Keeping Basket Lids Secure: Method 2" on page 57).

7. Make an 8" length of wrapped clothesline and zigzag stitch down the center. Insert the ends into the hole in the lid, forming a 1" loop handle on the outside. Knot the ends on the inside and secure with liquid glue and hand stitching. Glue seed beads over the knot with liquid glue for added interest.

8. Embellish the lid with beads (see "Embellishments" on page 63).

# HEART BASKET
# WITH FLAT LID

Finished Lid Measurements

| | |
|---|---|
| Height: ¾" | |
| Width: 10" | |
| Length at center: 7½" | |

A flat heart lid has short sides that come down over the top edge of the basket to hold the lid securely in place. The heart lid is constructed in the same manner as the heart basket, but the base is larger and the sides are shorter.

Refer to "Cutting Fabric Strips" on page 11 and "Wrapping Clothesline with Fabric Strips" on page 12 to prepare the wrapped clothesline for the project. Refer to "Basic Techniques" on page 10 as needed.

## Materials (for Both the Basket and Lid)

See "Basic Supplies" on page 8 and "Tools and Equipment" on page 9.

25 yards of clothesline

1 yard of fabric

Scraps of contrasting fabric for embellishment (optional)

Fusible web for appliqué (optional)

3 small, painted, wooden rings for embellishment (optional)

## How to Make the Heart Basket

Follow the instructions for "Making a U-Shaped Heart Base" on page 18, starting with a baseline measurement of 4". Bend the baseline in a U shape with 3¼" between the ends of the U. Stitch four flat rows around the baseline as for making a heart base. Remove the piece from the machine and trace the shape onto paper so the form can be duplicated for

the lid. Continue stitching wrapped clothesline around the heart base until it measures 7" x 4¼". Build up the sides around the base by stitching one row in angle position 2. Change to variation 2 of angle position 3 and continue until the basket measures 2¾" high. Taper off the clothesline. Reshape the basket if necessary. At the top edge, the finished basket measures 9" wide x 7" long through the center.

## How to Make the Matching Flat Heart Lid with Sides

1. Make a heart base using the drawing from the heart basket as a pattern for the starting shape. Continue adding rows of wrapped clothesline. When the lid size matches the heart basket opening, continue for one complete row, which adds an extra ½".

2. Build the sides around the base by stitching in variation 2 of angle position 3 for three rows. Try the lid on the basket and make any adjustments if necessary.

3. Taper off the clothesline to finish the lid.

4. Embellish the lid with contrasting heart appliqués cut from contrasting fabric (see "Fused Appliqué" on page 66). Edgestitch around the appliqués with thread that matches the basket. Stitch flat painted wooden rings to the appliqués, leaving multiple thread tails tied at the centers.

# FIGURE-EIGHT BASKET WITH FLAT LID

| Finished Lid Measurements |
| --- |
| Height of lid without handle: ¼" |
| Outer dimensions: 10" x 6¼" |

A flat lid is the easiest to make for a scallop basket and shows off the design lines nicely. The figure-eight lid is constructed in the same manner as the base for a figure eight-basket. However, for a snug fit, extra pieces of clothesline are stitched into the indented areas, so the finished lid outline becomes nearly oval, while the coiled interior maintains the figure-eight pattern.

Refer to "Cutting Fabric Strips" on page 11 and "Wrapping Clothesline with Fabric Strips" on page 12 to prepare the wrapped clothesline for the project. Refer to "Basic Techniques" on page 10 and "How to Make a Basic Figure-Eight Basket" on page 35 as needed.

## Materials (for Both the Basket and Lid)

See "Basic Supplies" on page 8 and "Tools and Equipment" on page 9.

28 yards of clothesline

1 ⅛ yards of fabric

1 ¼ yards of narrow cording, for handle

8" length of finished bamboo (or wood dowel), ½" in diameter, for handle

Two 12 mm flat beads for handle

## How to Make the Figure-Eight Basket

Make a figure-eight base by first starting with two 3½" round bases, and then outlining them with two rows of wrapped clothesline. Build up the sides around the base be adding one row in angle position 2, and then change to variation 2 of angle position 3. When possible, use variation 3, angle position 3, around the short ends and as the basket grows large enough. Use this position for the remaining rows. Continue until the basket measures 6" high. Taper off the clothesline. The finished basket measures 10½" x 7" across the top.

## How to Make the Matching Flat Figure-Eight Lid

1. Make a figure-eight base exactly the same size as the basket base by first starting with two 3½" round bases, and then outlining them with two rows of wrapped clothesline. Do not fill in the two small triangular gaps at the center where the round coils come together as they are used to help hold the bamboo handle in place. Continue adding rows as necessary until the lid reaches the correct size. Check the match between the lid and the lower basket often. The indented area on each side will be filled in later.

2. Taper off the clothesline.

3. Fill in the indented area on each side of the basket lid with strips of wrapped clothesline cut to fit and zigzag stitch in place.

4. If desired, apply fabric stiffener to the lid to help it stay level. Stitch beads to the interior of the basket to create a stopper for the lid (see "Keeping Basket Lids Secure, Method 1," at right).

5. Add a handle to the lid (see "Bamboo Rod Lid Handle" on page 62).

# KEEPING BASKET LIDS SECURE

For the projects in this book, I've used four basic methods for keeping lids secure on baskets. The first method is to stitch medium-sized beads to the inside of the basket so the lid can rest on the beads. This is a good method to use on flat lids. The second method is to whipstitch a row of wrapped clothesline to the inside of the lid, creating a lip, that will catch on the inside top edge of the basket and prevent the lid from slipping off. The third method is to stitch a row of wrapped clothesline to the interior of the basket, just below the upper edge, allowing a flat lid to rest on top of the lip. The fourth method is the disk-and-slit method. For this method, four small coiled disks are created and attached to the rim of the basket; then slits are created in the lid that correspond to the disks. The top half of the disks pokes up through the slits when the lid is in place, preventing the lid from slipping around.

## Method 1:
## Add Beads to the Inside of the Basket

Medium-sized beads can be used to create stoppers for the lid. For the basket shown here, I used square beads so that when several were placed together, they created a flat shelf that would support the lid. On the figure-eight basket, the lid is designed to rest just below the indented area on the basket sides. Plan the bead placement so the basket rests in the correct position. Stitch the beads in place at the desired locations.

## Method 2:
## Add a Lip to the Inside of the Lid

1. To find the correct position for the lip, place the lid on the basket, aligning the fronts, and then turn the lid and basket upside down. Push T-pins into the lid around the outer edge. Remove the basket and set the lid aside, with the pins intact.

2. Measure the circumference of the lid at the pin marks. Make a wrapped length of clothesline double this measurement plus 5" and stitch down the center. Pin the outermost side of the clothesline ¼" to the insides of the pins. Use liquid glue and hand tacking to secure the wrapped clothesline. Glue a second row of wrapped clothesline over the first.

## Method 3:
## Add a Lip to the Inside of the Basket

Measure the interior circumference of the basket at the desired placement height for the lip (just below the double binding on this basket). Make a wrapped length of clothesline a few inches longer than needed and stitch down the center. Glue and pin the wrapped clothesline at the desired placement height for the lip.

Trim off the excess clothesline and hide the join with a small piece of fabric that's glued and stitched in place.

## Method 4:
## Add Disks and Slits

1. Make four coiled disks, 1¾" in diameter, referring to "Making a Round Base" on page 14. Glue the disks equidistant apart around the rim of the basket so that half of each disk is above the rim.

2. Place the lid on the basket and mark slit openings in the lid that align with the disks on the basket; position the slits between rows of clothesline. Snip threads for one slit at time, making a 2" opening. Check that the disk fits into the slit. Repeat for all four disks. Zigzag stitch back over the snipped areas to reinforce the openings. Position the lid on the basket and insert the disks into the slits.

# HANDLES

Handles added to a project can be functional or purely decorative. They offer an opportunity to turn an ordinary basket into something special. This chapter is full of ideas for creating basket and lid handles. For baskets with lids, I usually omit the handles from the basket and use one handle on top of the lid instead. Choose a handle style and add it to the basket or lid of your choice. Purse handles are discussed on page 40.

Knotted side handles with beaded end coils accent a round striped basket. For handle instructions, see page 60.

## BASKET HANDLES

Consider handle options at the very start of your basket project. You may want to plan ahead and consider making any fabric changes at the point of handle placement so the changes won't be as noticeable.

Keep the following guidelines in mind when creating handles.

- Handles need to be sturdy enough so the basket won't bend or become floppy when lifted.

- Consider hiding the handle ends by tucking them underneath another portion of the project or by putting some embellishment over the end points.

- If making two matching side handles, measure carefully and style the handles so they match. The second handle should be a mirror image of the first.

- When attaching handles with hand stitching, use needle-nose pliers to help pull the needle through the layers. Avoid using needles with large eyes because they will leave holes in the fabric.

## Wrapped Clothesline Handles

To make the easiest handles, use the same clothesline that you've been working with all along. The wrapped clothesline can be easily twisted or coiled into endless designs to create unique handles.

To make a handle from a single length of clothesline, simply wrap fabric strips around the clothesline in the same manner as for the basket. Use a little more glue on the back of the fabric strips during the wrapping process to reduce fraying. Zigzag stitch along both edges or down the center of the clothesline to make a handle strip. If you're doing both edges, reduce the width of the zigzag stitch slightly from what was used on the basket so that the entire strip isn't covered with stitching. Form the strip into a loop or other shape and machine or hand stitch it securely to the basket concealing the ends.

**Loosely Coiled Handle.** For a smooth transition between a basket and a wrapped clothesline handle, stop stitching at the side of the basket when the basket reaches the desired height, but do not trim the excess clothesline. Move the clothesline away from the basket and zigzag stitch down the center for the desired distance (18" for the coiled handle on this basket). Cut the clothesline and remove the basket from the machine. Loosely coil the length of wrapped clothesline into a handle and pin to the basket, but leave space at the center for a large bead embellishment. Zigzag stitch down the center of a separate 18" length of clothesline, coil into a matching handle, and pin to the opposite side of the basket. Hand stitch the handles in place. Secure a layered bead embellishment to the center of each handle coil using hand stitches and liquid glue.

**Intertwined Wrapped-Clothesline Handles.** To make intertwined clothesline handles for a small basket, wrap a 40" length of clothesline with fabric and zigzag stitch down the center. The length of clothesline needed depends on the size of the basket and the planned design. Experiment with positioning the clothesline on the basket, coiling and looping it as desired. Create an intertwined loop design on one side of the basket, pinning the clothesline in place as you go. Curve the clothesline across the front side of the basket and create a similar intertwined clothesline handle on the opposite side. The handles don't need to match exactly. When you're finished with the second handle, curve the clothesline across the back of the basket to the starting point, tucking it under the handle to hide the end. Hand tack the entire length of clothesline in place. More wrapped clothesline was used to embellish the lid. See "Oval Basket with Raised Lid" on page 49 for more information.

**Oval Coiled Handle.** To create a handle for this 2"-high basket, I started with 12" of wrapped clothesline and made an oval base using a 1" baseline. I coiled and zigzag stitched the wrapped clothesline around the baseline for two rows, stopping on the left side. Then I carried the remaining clothesline over the top of the oval base in an arc, leaving a gap between the oval base and the arc. I attached the clothesline on the right side of the oval base, finished off at the bottom of the handle, and zigzag stitched over the arc. The handle was hand stitched and glued in place. A beaded design was stitched over the center of the oval baseline using size 6 seed beads and 6 mm and 8 mm wooden beads.

**Triple-Loop Handle.** This looped handle is ideal for smaller projects that don't require much strength. To create the triple-loop handle, stitch your basket, stopping at the desired height, but don't cut the clothesline. Move the clothesline away from the basket and zigzag stitch down the center for the desired distance (15" for the looped handle on this basket). Cut the clothesline and remove the basket from the machine. Shape the clothesline into a triple-loop and trim the excess. Pin the handle to the basket and hand stitch in place. Duplicate the handle shape with another piece of wrapped clothesline on the opposite side of the basket and stitch in place.

**Knotted Handle.** To make each of the side handles for this 5"-tall basket, a 44" length of clothesline was wrapped with fabric and zigzag stitched down the center. The wrapped clothesline was tied with multiple tight knots, starting 4" from one end. The knotting continues for about 7", with the excess clothesline formed into a 1¼"-diameter coil at the end. The 4" length at the starting end was folded in half to create a loop. The loops were stitched far enough into the inside of the basket to allow a couple knots to wrap over the basket rim. The coils were attached to the base of the basket and covered with small wooden beads hand stitched in place. Coat the handles with a fabric stiffener, if desired.

**Triple-Loop and Coil Handle.** A striking handle design is created on a synthetic fabric basket by making two small coiled loops at the rim of the basket and a large loop in between. About 32" of wrapped clothesline is needed for this handle to fit a 6"-tall basket measuring 8" in diameter across the top. For a little sparkle the fabric-wrapped clothesline is wound with strands of colored metallic thread. Make two matching handles, pin to the basket, and hand stitch in place.

**Reversed S-Coil Handles.** Wrap two separate 20" lengths of clothesline with fabric strips and zigzag stitch down the center of each. Make a round coil (two or three rows) from one length of clothesline and pin to the basket, leaving space at the center for a large round glass cabochon. Coil the remaining end of the clothesline in the opposite direction, leaving space for a small round glass cabochon at the center. Pin in place and secure with liquid glue and hand stitches. Use Crafter's Pick Fabric Glue to attach the glass cabochons in place. Repeat on the other side of the basket.

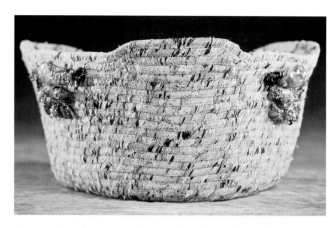

**Corner Handle Grips.** This style handle works well on a triangle basket. The instructions that follow are for a triangle basket. When the basket height is two rows or ½" from the desired finished height, stop stitching at the tape mark and remove it from the sewing machine. Cut and wrap three 3" lengths of clothesline and center one length on each corner of the basket at the upper edge. Zigzag stitch in place. Cut and wrap three 2½" lengths of clothesline and center one length on each corner over the previously stitched corner pieces. Zigzag stitch in place. Starting at the tape mark, continue stitching wrapped clothesline around the basket and over the handles for two more rows. Stop stitching 2" before you reach the tape mark on the last row. Taper off the clothesline to finish the basket. If there are any openings showing, add glued fabric to those areas and zigzag stitch over them.

## Flat Webbing Side Handles

Nylon or polyester webbing, covered with fabric, makes a sturdy handle on a basket. The handle strip covers both the inside and outside of the basket where it's attached, so it's ideal for baskets that have fabric changes because the handle can be used to conceal the changes.

1. Determine the desired length of the handle, measuring from the inside of the basket, up the desired distance above the rim, and down the outside of the basket. Cut two strips of webbing to this length.

2. From fabric, cut a strip 3" wide by the length of the webbing strip plus 1". Press ¼" of the fabric to the wrong side along one long edge of the strip.

Lightly apply glue stick to the webbing strip and position it on the wrong side of the fabric ⅞" from the remaining long edge.

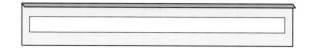

3. Wrap the long edges of the fabric strip over the webbing, positioning the folded edge on the top. Topstitch ⅛" from the edges and stitch one or two additional rows of stitching down the center as desired.

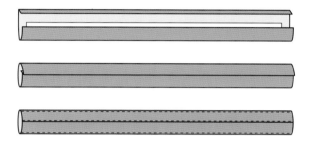

4. Fold ½" to the wrong side to conceal the ends and hand or machine stitch the handle to the basket.

**Flat Webbing Side Handle.** A contrasting strip was made for this handle with a ½" bias-tape maker and contrasting fabric. The strip was topstitched to the center of the handle before attaching the handle to the basket. A scrapbooking flower embellishment was glued over the end of the handle on each side. Another example of flat webbing side handles can be found on page 69.

# LID HANDLES

Before constructing a lid for a project, always consider the handle design so you know how large an opening to leave for the handle at the top of the lid. I usually make my lid handles from a length of wrapped clothesline that has been zigzag stitched down the center. To attach the handle, insert one end through the opening from the inside of the lid to the outside, allowing a 6" tail inside. Form a loop or any other desired design on the outside and then pass the end through the opening back to the inside of the lid. Tie a double knot and secure it with liquid glue and hand stitching.

**Ribbed Wooden Lid Handle.** Allow a ¼" opening at the center of the lid. Make a 10" length of wrapped clothesline and stitch down the center to secure. Tie a knot at one end, concealing the end, and insert three 1"-wide wooden craft wheels onto the other end. Secure the knot in place and glue the wooden wheels together. Insert the remaining end of the wrapped clothesline through the center of the lid from the top to the inside and trim to 2" long. Use liquid glue to secure the excess to the underside of the lid in a coiled shape. Hand stitch to secure.

**Multi-Loop Lid Handle.** For this handle, allow a ¾" opening in the center of the lid. Create a 38" length of wrapped clothesline. Thread the clothesline through the hole in the center of the lid from the inside to the outside, allowing a 6" tail inside. Create a 3" loop on the outside, and thread the clothesline back to the inside. Repeat to make seven loops. Tack the looped clothesline together on the inside of the lid. Tie the ends in a knot and secure inside with hand stitches and liquid glue. Arrange the loops on the outside as desired and secure with hand stitches and glue.

**Bamboo Rod Lid Handle.** For this handle, drill holes at the center of an 8" length of finished bamboo rod and also 1½" from each end. Then hand tack the rod to the lid, stitching through the drilled holes. Secure flat beads to the rod ends at the tacking points using hand stitching and glue. Insert the ends of a length of narrow black cording through the holes at the center of the lid from the underside. Tie the cording in knots, bunch up the knotted length, and hand tack it together to achieve the desired thickness and appearance. Push the ends back to the underside, trim them to 1" long, glue them in place, and glue a small scrap of fabric over them to conceal them. The bamboo rod for this handle came from recycling a bamboo rod place mat. You could also substitute a painted wood dowel for the bamboo rod.

# EMBELLISHMENTS

There are endless ways to embellish baskets. I often use beads, fusible appliqués, novelty yarns, wrapped clothesline strips, and double binding. Use the ideas shown on the following pages for inspiration in decorating your own baskets. More ideas are shown throughout the book.

Beaded tassels made this intricate-looking design easy. A beaded tassel with a broach-style topper was glued and hand tacked in place on two sides of the lid. An assortment of other beads embellishes the areas between the tassels. To make construction of the beaded dangle pieces easier and make them more durable, I strung an assortment of beads onto head pins and made a loop at the top of each with round-nose pliers (see photo, bottom left on page 64). Then I hand tacked the dangle pieces around the basket at the desired locations.

## BEADS AND BUTTONS

I often add beads and buttons to my projects because they work well for concealing the ends of handles. Sometimes I use beads to create a contrasting edge on basket rims. They also make great centers for flower appliqués. Secure beads and buttons in place with a strong liquid glue. When stitching beads directly to a project, I apply a small amount of Fray Check to the threads that hold the beads in place.

Black braid trim is glued and hand stitched over the rim of this scrappy round basket. A row of multicolored size 6 seed beads were strung on a double strand of thread and were hand tacked to the rim every three beads.

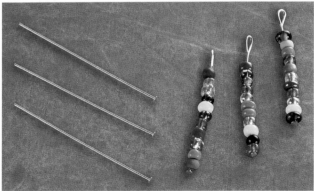

## SILK FLOWERS

Artificial flowers work well for accenting baskets. A good use for them is at the base of basket handles to conceal the ends.

The end of the basket handle shown above is concealed with a two-hole star button and 2" jewelry head pins strung with beads. Using head pins ensures a strong and straight beading line. String an assortment of beads onto head pins and make a loop at the top of each end with round-nose pliers. Securely stitch the dangle pieces in place at the end of the handle by stitching across the head pin in several places. Glue the button over the loops of the head pins and stitch a couple seed beads over the holes in the button.

A square basket edged with narrow satin ribbon features a cluster of silk flowers as a focal point. Clip the stems from several silk flowers to ¾" long and insert them from the right side of the basket through the row openings to form a cluster at the center front. Using needle-nose pliers, bend the stems so they can't be pulled out. Cut a piece of basket fabric large enough to cover the stems and secure in place with liquid glue.

# DIMENSIONAL-FABRIC EMBELLISHMENTS

To create both spiral streamers and dimensional flowers with curled edges, I use a technique that was taught by Joan Shay on the television program *Simply Quilts*. To start, fuse two layers of fabric wrong sides together with HeatnBond Ultra Hold iron-on adhesive, following the manufacturer's instructions. Then cut out the desired motifs. For spiral streamers, cut long strips from layers of fused fabric and tightly wrap the strips around a bamboo stick or wooden dowel. Spread the streamers out along the stick so all the areas are heated evenly. Set the shape by pressing with an iron and allow it to cool. Then hand stitch the streamers to the project. For flowers, cut out a flower shape and use liquid fabric glue or hand stitching to secure it to the project in the desired position. Curl the edges around a bamboo stick or wooden dowel and press with a mini-iron.

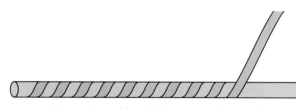

Wrap strips of fused fabric around a dowel and press to heat-set the shape.

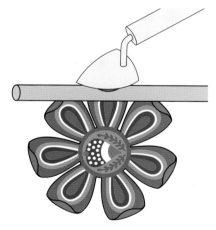

Roll the edges of flowers over a wooden dowel and press to heat-set the shape.

Dimensional streamers embellish the front of a child's purse. Tack streamers to a purse by stitching miniature colored buttons to each streamer at the desired points.

To make these small flower embellishments, triangles with sides measuring about 2" were cut from fabrics fused together with HeatnBond Ultra Hold iron-on adhesive. The corners of each triangle were loosely folded over and held in place with three beads stitched at the center.

Flower motifs were fused to contrasting fabric using HeatnBond Ultra Hold. The flowers were then cut out and the petals were curled. Two matching flowers were cut from contrasting fabric and fused to the basket with the dimensional flowers glued on top. Additional leaf and flower motifs appliquéd around the flowers to complete the embellishment.

# WRAPPED CLOTHESLINE EMBELLISHMENTS

Wrapped clothesline is easy to use for embellishments and can be knotted or manipulated into loops, coils, and other shapes. You can make a separate piece of wrapped clothesline to create a design or you can leave the wrapped clothesline attached to the basket when it reaches the desired height and use the attached strand to make a creative design.

To create the wrapped clothesline embellishment on this large basket, start with two 5-yard lengths of wrapped clothesline and zigzag stitch down the center. Make a knot at the center of each length, and then continue to make knots on each side of the center until the knotted area covers half the basket rim. Pin the center of the knotted piece to the center front of the basket at the upper edge. Continue pinning the knotted clothesline around the rim, stopping at the center of the short sides. Repeat with the other knotted piece on the back. Use the excess wrapped clothesline at each end to create loopy vertical patterns on the short ends of the basket. If more wrapped clothesline is needed, create another length and place the new end under the knotted clothesline or join two lines and cover with an embellishment. A variety of wooden beads and buttons were stitched over the clothesline to hold it in place. A large wooden giraffe embellishment was added to create a focal point.

# FUSED APPLIQUÉ

Fused appliqué works well on projects coiled from clothesline. Cut your own shapes or, for a very easy technique, cut a motif or design from printed fabric and fuse it to the project with fusible web. Use a mini-iron for hard-to-reach areas, like the inside bottom of a basket, and always follow the manufacturer's instructions for best results.

Two rectangles, cut from patterned fabric, were fused, one on top of the other, to the basket front. The appliqués are accented with French knots around the edges (see "French Knots," below). Gold beads add dimensional detail.

---

## French Knots

---

French knots are decorative embroidery stitches that are raised off the design surface. Use three strands of embroidery floss to make the knots.

| 1 | 2 |
|---|---|
| Twist the thread around the needle. | Insert the needle close to where the thread emerged. |

# JEWELED FABRIC ACCENTS

I created some interesting embellishments using a base of synthetic fabrics accented with metallic threads, craft wire, beads, glass cabochons, and paint. The pieces are heated with an embossing heat tool so the synthetic fibers melt slightly. To make each jeweled fabric accent, three or four pieces of shiny synthetic fabric in graduating lengths are rolled, largest to smallest, around a ½" length of clothesline. Metallic threads can be added, if desired. Hold the layers together temporarily with a binder clip and wrap with 26-gauge copper craft wire, removing the clip before heating. Pin the fabric accent to a pressing surface covered with an old towel or rag and heat with an embossing heat tool to slightly melt the synthetic fibers. Shield any area that you want to protect with a small spatula to prevent overheating. If desired, use a length of copper wire to secure a glass cabochon or a length of strung beads to the fabric piece. Highlight the piece with fabric paint if touch-ups are needed.

A triangle basket is embellished on each side with three jeweled fabric accents. Secure the embellishments to the basket with hand stitches and glue.

# NOVELTY YARNS

Novelty yarns work well for decorating a basket and for concealing attachment points or tapered clothesline ends. You can use a single variety or mix different types together.

Decorative twisted yarns create the edge finish on this basket. The yarns are held in place with beaded belt-loop style vertical accents. Short lengths of yarn decoratively sweep down over the basket front and are tacked in place with beading and hand stitching.

Decorative yarn is randomly swirled over the front and back of this oval basket and secured in place with liquid glue.

# DOUBLE BINDING

Sewing a double binding to the top edge of a basket can serve two purposes. It helps conceal the tapered end of the clothesline and when done in contrasting fabric, it becomes a decorative border.

1. Cut a 2" to 2½" strip across the width of the fabric and trim it to a length that is equal to the circumference of the edge you are binding plus 6". Make a 45°-angle cut on one end.

2. Fold and press ¼" of the angled end to the wrong side. Fold the binding in half lengthwise and press.

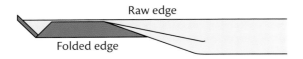

Raw edge

Folded edge

3. Align both of the raw edges of the binding with the upper outside edge of the project. Place the starting point where it will be least noticeable and pin. Starting 3" from the end, straight stitch ¼" from the long raw edges.

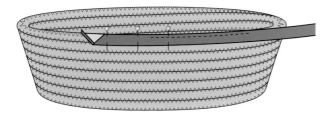

4. When you're almost back to the starting point, trim off the excess and insert the end of the binding into the fold at the beginning. Continue sewing the binding in place.

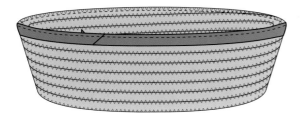

5. Turn the folded edge of the binding to the back or inside of the project, pin, and hand stitch in place.

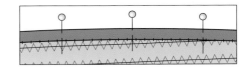

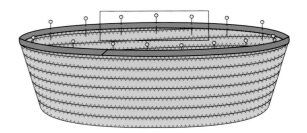

This coiled plate with a raised outer edge uses the main fabric for a double binding. The plate is made in the same manner as a base for a round basket (see "Making a Round Base" on page 14). To achieve the raised outer edge, the last two rows are stitched in angle position 1, and then the clothesline is tapered off (see "Tapering off the Clothesline" on page 24). A fused appliqué of puzzle pieces decorates the plate (see "Fused Appliqué" on page 66).

## Correcting a Bumpy Endpoint

If the ending spot of your clothesline is bumpy, insert a little batting or fabric into that spot before hand stitching the binding down. Another solution is to trim a small portion of the bump away, and then sew your binding.

# GALLERY

## Striped Basket with Flat Side Handles

Several fabrics were used to create the striped pattern on this round basket. Flat-webbing side handles were added to cover the fabric changes. The ends of the handles were concealed with a scrapbooking flower embellishment.

## Round Basket with Flat Side Handles and Scrappy Border

A scrappy border accents the top of this basket. Flat webbing handles hide the fabric change. The ends of the handles were embellished with star buttons and seed beads.

## Round Basket with Dimensional Flowers

Dimensional flowers created with HeatnBond Ultra Hold iron-on adhesive decorate the front of a small basket. To create a sturdy rim on this basket, I covered 1"-wide flat webbing with fabric and used it to wrap the basket rim.

## Small Basket Edged with Fibers and Beads

Twisted lengths of yarn embellish the rim of this small round basket. The fibers were held in place with vertical belt loop-style lines of seven seed beads. A spray of yarn and beads was added to the front to create a focal point.

## Tapered Round Basket

The upper edge of this large round basket was given its tapered appearance by stitching the last six rows in variation 3 of angle position 3. Double binding produces a nice finished edge around the rim.

## Batik Oval Basket

The wrapped clothesline used for this oval batik basket was continued onto the front of the basket and used to make a freeform embellishment, creating a continuous line of movement and eliminating the need to taper the end.

## Narrow Oval Basket on a Flat Base

This basket is one of my favorites. The plain purple fabric had no texture or print. As I wrapped the clothesline with fabric, I also wrapped purple #10 crochet thread over the wrapping to give it texture. This basket is too narrow to stand alone so I gave it an oval base. The basket was centered over the base and secured with liquid glue and hand stitching. Decorative yarn was lightly glued on at random, adding both texture and color.

### V-Shaped Oval Basket

The V shape of this basket comes from stitching the sides using variation 1 of angle position 3. To embellish this basket, I hand tacked a prestrung paper-and-wood-bead necklace around the basket, tacking the excess into a random design on the front.

### Large Oval Basket with Knotted Trim

Wrapped and stitched clothesline was used to create the knotted embellishment around the top edge and the dimensional clothesline decoration on the sides. The basket was further embellished with wooden beads and buttons of various shapes and sizes, including a large wooden giraffe.

### Large Multipurpose Basket

Whether it holds your latest craft project or today's mail, this basket is an attractive catchall. The 12" round base was reinforced with a grid of straight stitches and back tacking before the sides were formed. Because of the size, an acrylic table was used to support the project while stitching. Contrasting fabric was used for the top 2" of the basket, and then the top was turned down on itself to create a sturdy 1½"-wide contrasting border. The border was hand tacked in place.

## Small Painted Heart Basket

A small heart basket, created with a U-shaped base, was finished off with contrasting double binding. Lumiere paint was brushed on in a random pattern to add highlights to the nearly solid fabric. A doubled thread whipstitched around the binding adds texture to the rim.

## Medium-Sized Heart Basket

This medium-sized black-and-cream heart basket started with a U-shaped heart base. Black eyelash yarn was caught in the final row of zigzag stitching around the top edge to create a soft fuzzy finish.

## Synthetic V-Shaped Round Basket

With only a 2½" round base, this basket widens out by stitching the sides in variation 1 of angle position 3. For stitching successfully on the synthetic fabric, which featured metallic dots, I used a ballpoint needle. Wrapped clothesline straight stitched down the center was used to make the looped edging around the rim.

## Pyrex-Lined Halloween Basket. From the collection of the Chris Breier Family.

This Halloween basket is ready for treats. A glass- or plastic-lined basket allows more possibilities for using the basket. Buy a brand-name liner so if it gets broken you can easily find a replacement. To make a basket to match a liner, create a base of the same size and add sides that match the angle of the liner sides. Test the fit of the liner in the basket often during construction. Finish off at the correct height. Halloween motifs are fused to the basket front and blanket stitched around the edges.

## Round Synthetic Basket with a Frayed Rim

A lightweight synthetic fabric with flowing lines in caramel, brown, and cream was used for this small round basket. The selvage had a long frayed edge so it was saved to wrap the clothesline for the top finished edge.

## Caden's Camouflage Basket

My grandson, Caden Breier, asked for a basket of his own. Camouflage fabric with army buttons and insignias was just what he wanted. The basket has fairly straight sides because it was large enough to encircle the top of the machine. The badges were secured with liquid fabric glue and hand stitching. Caden loves it!

## Tall Multicolored Vase

Although I didn't care for the pattern in this bargain fabric, the colors were right so I turned it into a wonderful vase-shaped basket. The upper edge flares out because it was stitched in angle position 4. The 9" basket is embellished with metallic trim and colorful glass beads.

## Scrappy Plate with Tree Appliqué

This 11½" plate was divided in half with creamy scraps wrapped for the sky and three other fabrics wrapped for a meadow and flower garden. The tree and the grouping of leaves were fused to the plate. A narrow zigzag stitch secures the edges. The red apples are HotFix Swarovski crystals from Kandi Corp and were applied with a heat applicator.

## Vertical Wrapped-Clothesline Purse with Appliqué Design

Design elements were cut from several different fabrics backed with fusible web. The pieces were arranged on the shiny side of a sheet of freezer paper, pressed together lightly, and then transferred as one piece to the purse front. The piece was fused in place using a pressing sheet to protect the fabric. The individual pieces were edgestitched for added security before the side panels were added. The handle was created by zigzag stitching rows of unwrapped clothesline together, and then repeating the process for a separate second layer. The handle layers were then stitched together between the rows of clothesline. Scribbles paint was brushed over the handle and worked into the clothesline. A ribbon and yarn embellishment decorates one side of the handle and beads were stitched to the opposite side.

## Banded Carryall Purse

Three fabrics are used to give this purse a striped design. The 1"-wide wrapped-webbing straps are glued and tacked from the bottom to the top giving the purse extra strength. Narrow fabric-covered cording is used to make the closure bows. They are tacked to the back strap at the upper edge of the purse and tied in front.

## Scrap Fabric Shoulder Bag

This versatile shoulder bag has a unique scrappy look. Each row was wrapped with a different fabric. Color changes were made on the back of the purse where the strapping hides it. The strapping was covered with three rows of clothesline encased in fabric. The fabric-encased clothesline strip was backed with grosgrain ribbon. The closure was made from a piece of bamboo rod with a drilled center hole. Thread a knotted nylon cord through the hole from the front to the inside of the purse and secure. Thick elastic hair bands stitched to the back of the purse wrap over the top and encircle the bamboo rod.

## Child's Purse

This simple purse was made for my five-year-old granddaughter, Katie Breier. It was constructed from two round bases that were attached to an all-in-one strapping piece that also becomes the purse sides and bottom. Three strips of wrapped clothesline were zigzag stitched to a narrow length of fabric with the raw edges folded in to create the strapping piece. It was attached to the round bases with Mighty Mendit adhesive and a few hand stitches. The front of the purse was embellished with colorful spiral streamers and miniature buttons. The top edge of each round base piece was folded over, glued, and hand tacked in place. For an adult version, simply make the round bases larger and choose a suitable fabric.

## Urn-Style Round Basket

The top and bottom of this urn are separate components made with the same size base. They were joined together with liquid glue and hand stitching. The top portion has a V shape because the sides were stitched in variation 1 of angle position 3. The last four rows were stitched in angle position 4. The wrapped clothesline embellishment was created with 60" of wrapped and zigzag-stitched clothesline. To make it pop off the background better, I added color to the wrapped clothesline with Shiva Paintstiks and 3-D glitter paint. For added support, two rows of wrapped clothesline were added to the inside edge of the small base. The base was also treated with a fabric stiffener.

# RESOURCES

Having the right type of clothesline is important for the success of your project. Look for cotton clothesline that is $3/16$" to $7/32$" in diameter. It can be poly-reinforced cotton as long as the clothesline is soft, very flexible, and has no hard center core. Ask a store associate to open a package so that you can check the clothesline before you buy it. Never buy plastic clothesline or the colored all-poly clothesline. Usable clothesline is often located in the laundry or farm-supplies section of a store. Below is a listing of brands I have tested and nationwide stores that carry them.

My preferred clothesline is Whitney Design brand #04800. It's available in a 100' package of $3/16$" poly-reinforced cotton clothesline. It has been available at ShopKo Stores or through my business, Susan's Stitches (5080 Island View Drive, Oshkosh, WI 54901; email skbreier@new.rr.com; website www.susansstitches.com).

Mainstays Home brand cotton clothesline comes in a 100' package of $3/16$" clothesline. It is available at Wal-Mart.

Wellington brand cotton clothesline is available in $7/32$", $9/64$", or $1/4$" diameters. You can find this at Menards, True Value, or Aubuchon Hardware. The smaller-diameter Wellington clothesline or twine works great for embellishments.

Ace Hardware cotton clothesline is available in 50' or 100' packages of $7/32$" clothesline. You'll need to buy 100' in case you decide to make a large basket or add a lid.

Try asking your favorite quilt or fabric store to stock some clothesline. If they carry this book they might be willing to carry the clothesline also.

# ABOUT THE AUTHOR

Susan discovered that taking life easy wasn't all that she had hoped it would be after an early retirement. When the hectic pace of raising two boys with her husband, Jeff, and working outside of the home for many years was over, winding down seemed unnatural. She needed more out of life than total relaxation. Taking on a new challenge was the answer.

Sewing and crafts of all types had been an interest since childhood and it was time to rekindle her love of the creative process. New doors opened after she was exposed to the quilting world. By joining Lakeside Quilters in Oshkosh, Wisconsin, and Darting Needles Quilt Guild in Appleton, Wisconsin, her interest grew with each meeting. She was hooked and loved every minute of it.

With her quilting came the mounting containers of fabric. Scraps were building up but she couldn't part with the leftover pieces.

She started making projects with fabric-wrapped clothesline and spent her free time perfecting the method. Soon other people were interested in learning how to make the projects. With encouragement she agreed to write a book. Writing was something that was never in her life's plan, but "When you love doing something you just want to share the excitement," she explained. *It's a Wrap* was released in August of 2006.

What a whirlwind of activities followed. Her method was an absolute favorite of many. Emails arrived saying "thank-you" from ladies who were overjoyed with the method and were stitching up a storm. Teaching, vending, writing magazine articles, and traveling to shows soon followed. In addition, she allowed her method to be used in Kenya so displaced women and their children could better support themselves. The women of Kenya had always made wonderful baskets and American volunteers wanted them to try Susan's lids and embellishments.

With the publication of this second book, Susan is busier than ever trying to meet the demand for items in her unique style. She's very thankful to have discovered a new purpose for her life that also brings joy to others. Her prayers have been answered.